# THE HEALTHY CHRISTIAN:

## AN APPEAL TO THE CHURCH.


BY HOWARD CROSBY,

PASTOR OF FOURTH-AVENUE PRESBYTERIAN CHURCH,
NEW YORK.

AMERICAN TRACT SOCIETY,
150 NASSAU-STREET, NEW YORK.

# PREFACE.

I ADDRESS this book to Christians; to those who, being in Christ Jesus, walk not after the flesh, but after the Spirit. It is an effort to stir up pure minds by way of remembrance.

The world's way of making a good Christian is to lead the Christian into conformity with itself and reduce Christianity to a matter of ethics, and perhaps physiology. The Bible way is to separate the Christians from the world unto Christ, according to the grand truth that Christianity is not a code or system for mind and body, but a divine life, a life which is directly antagonistic to the world's life. The church is lamentably allied to the world through the agencies of wealth and fashion; and it becomes us to sound an alarm for Christ's sake, and remind the people of God of their true privileges and responsibilities. Under the impulses of earthly ambition for place and riches, a tendency has been developed to bring down all religion to the low level of a respectable naturalism, and thus dishonor God's revelation. Sincerity (a sincerity, too, which scorns all seeking after God) is considered quite as good as regeneration; and a man is counted a Christian who utterly ignores the person, work, and word of Christ. It is considered a beautiful liberality to put Mohammed, Vishnu, the Virgin Mary, and Ormuzd on a par with Jesus, and to count science, reason, poetry, and revelation as equal authorities. This is the prevailing style of religion that we find in the newspapers which have to cater to every sort of taste, and which, therefore, deemed an undefined *olla podrida* the most suitable form of religion for journalism. Weak souls are snared by this popular and human thing, and the *vox populi* becomes to them the *vox Dei.* The true voice of God in his revealed word is first neglected, then despised, then assailed.

The only remedy for this evil is for each individual Christian to renew his application to that word, and, under its guidance, to come out and be separated from the world at whatever cost of social position, political honors, or pecuniary fortune. We are to trust in the Lord and go forward, and we shall find in him our exceeding great reward.

CONTENTS

## CHAPTER VII.



## CHAPTER VIII.



## CHAPTER IX.



## CHAPTER X.

THE

# HEALTHY CHRISTIAN.

## CHAPTER I.

### THE GENERAL VIEW.

"THAT THEY MAY BE SOUND IN THE FAITH."

THE old English word "*sound*," like the Greek ὑγιαίνωσιν of this passage in Paul's epistle to Titus, is equivalent to the ordinary English "healthy." The apostle urges his representative in Crete to secure healthiness in the faith to the Cretan Christians. Titus 1:13.

As to the *faith* he speaks of, it is too often referred merely to doctrine. Faith in the gospel sense has two complementary parts; the one is the objective truth revealed by God in his word, and the other is the soul's grasp of that truth, the personal appropriation and absorption of the divine doctrine. We have no right to use the words "the faith" as meaning an external creed. The article before the word does not give us that right, for in the next chapter to the one from which we have derived our text, we find the aged men are to be sound in *the* faith, in *the* charity, and in *the* patience—as the Greek has it. Now as *the* charity and *the* patience refer to a condition of heart, so does *the* faith. We have corrupted the word in our usage, and talk of a man's faith, when we refer only to the intellectual theses that he has chosen, for any purpose whatever, to write on his standard. We must correct this error, when we read the Bible. Soundness in the faith does not mean orthodoxy, but a healthiness of the soul in its acceptance of the pure truth of God. The subjective side of the phrase receives the greater emphasis.

This healthiness in faith, as subjective, is a

personal matter. It cannot be affirmed of an aggregate, a community, without regard to the individuals composing the community. If the faith were in externals, it might be so affirmed. Rites, ceremonies, and emblazoned formularies would satisfy all the conditions. A church composed of devils might in this way be sound in the faith. But a healthy church is that which consists of healthy Christians.

What, then, is a *healthy Christian?* That is the important question which we shall attempt to answer in the following pages. The very word suggests a comparison of soul with body, and in pursuing this comparison we may, perhaps, best reach our end.

The most natural inference which we draw from the word and its use by the apostle is that there are sickly Christians. Christ, the great Physician, came to give health to these souls, but somehow they have not received the boon in its fulness. The remedies have been sufficient, and the Physician has been infinitely skilful. The fault, therefore, must lie in the patients. Either they have not conformed to the prescriptions, or they have counteracted their effect by inconsistent additions, or they have permitted evil influences to act upon them, and thus thwarted the sufficient help afforded them.

The inference from the apostle's words is fully sustained by observation. Nothing can be more apparent than the difference between the New Testament Christian and the average Christian of to-day. If we draw a portrait of a Christian from the descriptions furnished us in Scripture, we have a man separated *from the world,* abjuring its habits of life, its aims and ambitions, its maxims and methods, its pomps and pleasures, and separated *unto Christ;* finding joy unspeakable in communion with Him, serving Him in His cause of grace, using opportunities and means to do good after His pattern, making all his alliances and intimacies with Christ's people, and living in the happy expectation of a home with God. But if we draw the portrait of the average Christian, we have a man who makes his partnerships and close relationships with a Christless world, assumes the world's style of living, engages his attention and time in the plans and purposes of this short life, avoids any separating token from the world lest he mar his worldly prospects, never speaks of Christ except by a violent effort, is seen in questionable transactions, brings up his family for earthly prizes, and dreads death and eternity. These outward differences, that are noticeable at a glance, could be paralleled by the differences in spiritual feeling and principle. In the one case are profound meditation on God's revealed truth, a handling of the precious promises, a cheerful study of God's daily providence, a constant inhaling of heavenly grace as of the odors of sweet flowers all along the road, and the joyous feeling of growing strength in the way of Christ; while on the other are cares of property and preferment, envies and jealousies towards the more successful, conscience-struggles against the calls of God, grief or vexation at earthly disappointments, and a general dissatisfaction and restlessness.

The average Christian thus described, is sickly. By hypothesis he is a Christian, but he has just enough life in his soul not to be entirely dead. His spiritual life corresponds to the physical life of a man in a fever, and with ulcers breaking forth upon his flesh, racked with cough, tormented with headache, or lost, perhaps, in stupor. He lives, but what a life!

It is a melancholy and alarming fact that vast numbers of Christians are of this type, bringing reproach on the name they bear, and counteracting the blessed invitations of the gospel by the sad specimens of Christianity they exhibit in themselves.

The conviction forces itself upon us that the scars of these inconsistencies must remain on the soul for ever. Heaven is not a dead level. Grades mark differences of character there, and the elements of that gradation we may not anticipate. In mysterious consonance with heaven's happiness must be the different positions of those who have persisted even to the last in frittering away the gifts of grace by shameful dallying with a false world. We cannot but believe that the Nethinim foreshadowed a class in heaven. Surely there are some Gibeonitish Christians who will be hewers of wood and drawers of water in the Promised Land. It will not do for these sickly Christians to say that when death comes, it will be all the same. It will not be all the same. The consequences of their worldliness will go with them to all eternity. How that will be is not for us to say, but the Scripture is very plain that a wilful neglect of Christian privileges meets its appropriate reward. We will not endeavor to interpret the following words of our Lord, but they mean something: "That servant, which knew his Lord's will and prepared not himself, neither did according to his will, shall be beaten with many stripes."

This subject is one of the most important that can appeal to a Christian's mind. It is the question of his own relation to the Lord Jesus and his work of grace. It is the question of growth and evangelization. It is the question of personal truth and righteousness. One grand reason why the whole world is not now the Lord's by faith is the personal worldliness of Christians. Not one Christian in ten testifies as he should for his Master; not one in a thousand is a "burning and shining light." The whole church, which ought to be electric at every point, each member surcharged from the Holy Spirit, has a feeble, fragmentary efficiency, and shows the activity of a rheumatic patient who has a few fingers free. The revival of the church is the first question before Christians to-day. Let the joy of Christ's salvation be understood by the church, and then she may teach transgressors God's ways, and behold sinners converted to the truth in Jesus. It is Christians that need conversion, just as poor Peter did; and the longer they defer it, the harder a road will they make it. Oh, what a sight this is for the angels! the Lord Christ is crying out his heavenly wares, and his own people will not buy them, though an open treasury is theirs to use, given them for this end.

That we may minister to the sick church, let us examine what a healthy Christianity is. Two great systems of efficiency are found in the human body, the blood-system and the nerve-system. The heart is the reservoir of the former and the brain of the latter. Through the blood the food is assimilated to the body, and thus the body is constantly preserved and maintains its integrity. The food supplies the blood, and the air we inhale is a constant purifier of the blood so supplied. On this blood-system depends all else in the body, so that the Scripture statement has a literal force: "The life of the flesh is in the blood." Lev. 17:11. By a marvellous network of arteries, capillaries and veins the blood is circulated through every portion of the human frame, and is perpetually engaged in its work of repairing the body's waste and fostering its growth. If the blood lose in quantity or quality, or if the circulation be impeded, the body at once fails, weakness and disease invade it, and the *life* is so far marred. Hence the main effort of the physician is to restore the efficiency of the blood, and when this is established, the "vis medicina naturæ"—nature's restorative energy—accomplishes the cure. The poison of the viper does not affect the body until it is taken into the blood, and conversely the purification of the blood is the healing of the man.

Now if we regard the spiritual man, we find an analogue to the blood-system of the body in Christ himself. Christ is our life, just as in the body "the life is in the blood." It is as Christ permeates the soul in its every department and function that the Christian meets the requirements of his new nature. *His* personal contact with the soul builds it up and prevents its decay, supplying its ever-recurring wants. *He* is "made unto us wisdom and righteousness and sanctification," as well as redemption; just as, in the body, bone and sinew and cartilage are derived from the blood, the whole man being built up from this source. There is no part of the spiritual man for which Christ is not the sufficient supply. What are called the graces of the Spirit are but the applications of Christ. The reason of their name "fruit of the Spirit" (Gal. 5:22 and Eph. 5:9,) we shall consider hereafter. What is our spiritual joy but the result of the consciousness of Christ's saving presence? What is our spiritual patience but the rest and contentment which spring from the same source? What is our Christian love but the touch of Christ's love reacting in us? See in what a comprehensive way the cross of death furnished us with life! Understand how Christ is "all and in all!" Behold how without Christ spiritual life is impossible! A soul without Christ is as a body without blood. It is a dead soul, however you may give it the semblance of life by art. The Christless soul is as truly destitute of spiritual life as the beast is destitute of rational life, and the vegetable is destitute of animal life. The vegetable lives, but it lives on a lower plane than the beast; the beast lives, but it lives on a lower plane than the man; the man lives, but he lives on a lower plane than the saint. So when we say that a soul not sainted by Christ's presence is dead, we do not say it has no kind of life, but that it has no spiritual life—no particle of that highest life for which God designed it. In this true and sublime view, it is *dead*. The spiritual life consists in Christ everywhere active in the soul, as the blood is in the body. Of course this cannot be a Christ *speculative*, or a Christ *sentimental*. Neither speculation nor sentiment is a spring of life. Nor can it be a *human* Christ, who shall cause a divine life in the soul. It is not an *exemplary* Christ or a *sympathizing* Christ, but an indwelling, energizing Christ, who must form the very blood of the soul, his example and his sympathy being real but secondary to his essential union with us. It is in this way the Christian says, "1 live, and yet not I, but Christ liveth in me." Gal. 2:20. So we can understand the wonderful words of the prayer of Jesus, "As thou, Father, art in me and I in thee, that they also may be one in us." "I in them and thou in me." "That the love wherewith thou hast loved me may be in them and I in them." John 17:21, 23, 26. What is it that fills the Christian heart with peace and causes it to rejoice in the fulness of a heavenly hope? Is it its holiness? Is it the record of the earth-life? Is it even God's mercy and love? Is not "*Christ in us* the hope of glory"? Is not Christ dwelling in the soul and moving it in its life, as the blood dwells and moves in the veins, the cause and pledge of our glory, the true basis of our joy and hope?

It is this which separates true Christianity from all religions of mere creed and law, as far as the heaven is separated from the earth. The Christian, to whom *duty* is the idea of religion, has not begun to understand the principle of his spiritual life. Duty has no part in the Christian scheme except as it proceeds from the Christ-life of the soul. In any other light it is self-righteousness and heathenism. Hence the cry of God to the soul is not "Do," but "Believe;" and this leads to another branch of thought.

The blood is formed in the body from the food eaten. So Christ is formed in us from the Holy word accepted by faith. Faith is thus the mouth of the soul, in accordance with that exhortation of the Lord, "Open thy mouth wide and I will fill it." Ps. 81:10. We receive Jesus through the word. He that feeds on God's word has Christ formed in him. The written word introduces the personal Word. And as the body cannot eat once for all, but must eat daily, so God's word must be daily used in order that the Christ-life be sustained in our souls. The disuse of the word is a starvation process for the Christian. The first Psalm describes the blessed man as one meditating day and night in God's revealed truth; and the 119th Psalm is a varied reiteration of the paramount importance of a constant feasting upon the same holy word. It is by reason of the waste and losses of the body that the blood must be ever renewed by food, and it is by reason of the waste of the soul, its frailty and weakness through sin, that Christ must be ever supplied anew to it by the aliment of the word. From these considerations we may see the relation of the Bible to the Christian. It is a vital relation. His intelligence is in question only in a subordinate way. His heart, his life, his inner being of will and motive and affection are directly interested. The intellectual elements of the Bible are only valuable as, by enlightening the mind, they open the heart. The Bible is life-giving only as Christ is in it, and the reading of the Bible is life-receiving only as Christ is accepted in it. It is faith that alone makes this appropriation. It is the trust of a child listening to its father's voice, and by a natural instinct storing its treasures of truth in the chambers of the soul. It is a process of the tenderest and truest affections. The soul has passed beyond the region of doubts and criticism when it has thus learned to feed on the word. It has tasted the heavenly manna and knows its freshness and sweetness.

A dark thought has to be inserted here. It is possible for the Christian, by yielding to worldly influences, to lose his relish for this celestial food. "Our soul loatheth this light bread" was said of provision from God's own table. There is no better test of a healthy piety than an appetite for the Bible. It shows the soul's fondness for Christ and its longing to sustain the constant experience of Christ within. It shows that it knows the way to do this, and makes a habit of its privilege. The Bible study of faith is the making blood for the soul, the supply of Christ's efficiency to the spiritual life.

## CHAPTER II.

### THE GENERAL VIEW—OTHER MEANS OF LIFE.

CONSIDER next some other features in the analogy between physical and spiritual life.

In the body the blood is kept pure by the respiratory organs, supplying *fresh oxygen* with every breath. Without this the avenues of life would be clogged and the food would prove a minister of evil and death.

Now it is remarkable how constantly the teachings of Christ and his apostles urge Christians to association. They are not to forsake the assembling of themselves together; the very name of church (ἐκκλησία) denotes an assembly. A special blessing is given to the gathering together of Christians to pray; they are to meet together on the first day of the week; they are spoken of as a *company;* they are to refresh and comfort one another; in short, the whole New Testament views the Church of Christ as a band of brethren gathered together and separated from the world. This Christian communion acts to the individual Christian as the fresh air acts upon the body. It is by this that the faith of the soul is preserved from becoming false or fantastic, and the graces are maintained in truth.

Isolation begets selfishness, and selfishness is the bane of faith. The truth of God in us needs a perpetual contact with that truth in others in order to preserve its purity. The plant shut out from light and air withers or has a sickly growth; and the Christianity that foregoes the communion of the saints loses its tone and is a prey to spiritual fungi. We cannot find high types of Christian life either in the hermit's cell or in the haunts of fashion. The Christianity found in either lacks oxygen. It has not breathed a healthy atmosphere. Asphyxia is threatened in each case: in the one case by breathing, or trying to breathe, in a vacuum, and in the other by breathing in an impure air. The same divine physician who has prescribed for us the food of the word, has also prescribed a Christian communion as a regulator of that word's effects in the heart. The blood is indebted not only to the food but to the air we breathe; and our possession of Christ in us is dependent not only on the truth we accept, but on the company we keep. A clear conviction and childlike faith, with the elasticity and vigorous glow belonging to them, may be followed by a sad experience of doubts and fears, of sloth and stupidity, of waywardness and wandering, all by reason of the false associations permitted by the converted heart. The sources of truth are kept open to the soul, but they are counteracted in their efficacy by the constraints of evil associations. "I read my Bible and I pray," say many, "but I obtain no relief." The trouble is not in the food, but the air. The social intimacies of the world nullify all that the Bible and prayer might do. No food will keep a man healthy in a fetid cellar or amid the fumes of a match-factory. The cry to a believer should be as much "Look to your lungs" as "Look to your stomach." Cultivate a Christian society, as well as study prayerfully God's word, if you would have Christ in you as the blood of your soul in a pure and unimpeded current.

But there is still another important consideration. We are wont, and rightly, to couple *exercise* with air, when we prescribe for debilitated bodies. We know the breathing itself is performed better when the body is properly excited by motion; that the lungs play to their full extent, and every corner of their functionary surface is brought into use. We know, too, that by exercise, desirable mechanical as well as chemical changes are superinduced in the system, the body throwing off its incumbrances, while its tissues are strengthened by a more equal distribution of its humors. So the soul needs *its* exercise. It must put forth its activities in its social opportunities. The social benefits will be rightly received and their virtues enhanced by this. A Christian must not be a passive recipient among his fellows, but he must improve his recipiency by activity. It is as we exercise our graces that they grow. Christian society furnishes us with a pure air to breathe, but we must be stirring amid it, if we would gain all its advantages in ourselves. We must drink it into the lungs of our spiritual man by cheery exercise. Christian work ought to be no more irksome than the activity of a healthy body on a crisp autumn morning. By Christian work we mean any use of the graces God has given us. The sympathies, the encouragements, the helps, the instructions, which we may bestow on others; the self-restraint, the love, the patience, the forbearance, which we may cultivate in ourselves; the faith, obedience, hope, and filial affection, which we may foster toward God—all classify themselves under the head of Christian work, that active exercise by which we make the most of Christian society, and render it fully the accompaniment of the spiritual food which the word furnishes to the soul.

This sketch of the soul's blood-system may suffice for our purpose. A few words respecting the soul's nerve-system follow. The nerves of the body give sensation to every part, and thus arouse responsive action to every touch from without. They are, besides, the connecting link between body and mind, running in this way into a region where we cannot trace them. A peculiar mystery belongs to them in this their relation to the higher being. In both these relations the nerves are the watchful superintendents of the whole frame. The blood-system could not exist a moment without the nerve-system. It would forget to perform its functions if the nerves did not ever give their ready signals. It is through the nerves, too, the senses act. Sight and hearing, smelling and taste would not be, but for nerves which make them possible and efficient.

All our discriminations in the material world are made through the nerves. We know the difference between the sweet odor of the rose and the foul fumes of mephitic vapor—between the fair, sunny landscape, with stream and mountain, and the dingy aspect of a smoky factory-town in a rain-storm; between the delicious flavor of a peach and the bitter taste of wormwood—only by the action of our nerves.

Now, if we turn to the spiritual man, we find an element of the spiritual life which exactly answers to the nerve-system. It watches over the whole life. It makes it sensitive to the impact of the spiritual world without; it suggests the soul's responsive activity; it connects the soul with the mysterious infinite by bonds that transcend description and definition, and it gives the spiritual man his powers of discernment between good and evil. This is the Spirit of God in the conscience and consciousness; (the Greeks had one word, συνείδησις, for both.) The Spirit of God is resident in the believer; hence he is called the temple of the Holy Spirit. 1 Cor. 6–19; 2 Cor. 6–16. It is from this source come the spiritual perceptions and discriminations of the regenerated soul. Look at Paul's remarkable language: "God hath revealed [these mysteries] unto us by his Spirit; for the Spirit searcheth all things, yea, the deep things of God. For what man knoweth the things of a man, save the spirit of man which is in him? Even so the things of God knoweth no man, but the Spirit of God. Now we have received, not the spirit of the world, but the Spirit which is of God, that we might know the things which are freely given us of God. . . . . . But the natural man receiveth not the things of the Spirit of

God, for they are foolishness unto him; neither can he know them, because they are spiritually discerned. But he that is spiritual judgeth all things, yet he himself is judged of no man. For who hath known the mind of the Lord, that he may instruct him? But we have the mind of Christ." 1 Cor. 2:10–16. This indwelling of God the Spirit in the believer's soul is too often explained away as figurative, because incomprehensible. The presence of our own souls within our bodies is incomprehensible; how can we expect to comprehend the indwelling of the Divine Spirit? But the incomprehensible is true and demands our faith, and the recognition of God within us is the grandest secret of Christian growth. "Know ye not your own selves," says the Apostle, "how that Jesus Christ is in you?" 2 Cor. 13:5. And so the Spirit is affirmed to dwell equally within us. "If any man have not the Spirit of Christ," (called the Spirit of God immediately before,) "he is none of His; and if Christ be in you, the body is dead because of sin, but the spirit is life because of righteousness. But if the Spirit of him that raised up Jesus from the dead dwell in you, he that raised up Christ from the dead shall also quicken your mortal bodies by his Spirit that dwelleth in you." Rom. 8:9–11. Here the Spirit is called both the Spirit of God and the Spirit of Christ, and has a veritable indwelling in the human body and soul as the soul's true life, and yet is distinct from Christ dwelling in us. We may talk of it as an influence or an emotion or a tendency; but it is more than those. It is one who can bear witness with our spirit, (ver. 16,) help our infirmities and make intercession for us, (ver. 26,) and that is what an influence or emotion or tendency could not do. No! let us meet the stupendous fact fully. It is truly God in us. As we have said, the Holy Spirit in us is the nerve-system of the spiritual life. It is he who watches and witnesses within us, and by his holy influences keeps the truth in us pure and energetic. It is he who who gives that wisdom of perception by which the Christian soul knows the truth from a lie, and almost instinctively separates the good from the evil. It is he who checks and corrects, warns and exhorts, encourages and soothes the soul in its various exercises and experiences. Christ is in us as the source of growth and the maintainer of life, and the Holy Ghost is in us as the communicator of the life-principle, the furnisher of spiritual sensation and its discriminating power. In point of time there is no priority in the reception of Christ and the Holy Spirit by the soul, but in logic there is. It is the Holy Spirit who regenerates, who quickens the dead soul to a new birth, and thus enables it to accept Christ and all his efficiency. Born of the Spirit, the new-born soul feeds on the sincere milk of the word and thus Christ is developed within. The whole is one work of God with the soul, but our finite minds are obliged to analyze and look at it in parts.

The nerve-system of the body is preserved in health by the same means which preserve the blood-system. If the blood is kept pure and vigorous, the nerves, like the sinews and the muscles, will be kept in healthy exercise. So in the Christian soul, it is Christ in us, in his truth and fulness, through a constant communion with the word and with Christ's own redeemed ones, that will ever preserve our conscience from numbness and our judgment from error. So our active conscience and correct judgment will react upon us in making Christ more clear and satisfactory to the soul. The two systems act and react upon one another. There is blood in the brain and there are nerves in the heart. No human mind can draw the line between the work of Jesus and the work of the Spirit in the converted soul. The interlacings and implications of both among motives, perceptions, affections and will are a mystery and must be a mystery. But we may make the general analysis, that we have made, in considering Jesus Christ as forming the life-blood of the soul and the Holy Spirit as forming the nerve-power of the same, in its new condition as begotten of God and endowed with a new nature. We may, in general, place Christ in the region of the affections and will, and the Holy Spirit in the region of the conscience and judgment, and yet we know well that this is but a crude approximation to the truth.

A sound faith (or a healthy faith) is, then, a free and regular action of these divine elements in us, a "fulness of God," in accordance with that prayer of Paul regarding the Ephesians: "that he would grant you, according to the riches of his glory, to be strengthened with might by his Spirit in the inner man, that Christ may dwell in your hearts by faith ....... that ye might be filled with all the fulness of God." A sound faith is a faith which makes Christ, the life of the soul, to be felt in every fibre of our being, giving a glow to all and conforming all to itself; and in which the Holy Spirit is ever the inspirer and guide of this soul-life. A sound faith is thus eminently a divine thing. It has no earthly contents or earthly support. It anticipates the heavenly citizenship and lives here an exotic, a stranger and foreigner. It is no product of philosophies or societies or poetry. Nor can it be gauged by men's natural judgments, however refined and educated they may be. Men (unconverted and unregenerate men) cannot, therefore, prescribe for a faith, that it may become sound. They are constantly attempting it, but none of their nostrums ever reach the seat of the disease. Nor can men without effort expect to gain a sound or healthy faith. "Giving all diligence" is the apostolic precept. (2 Pet. 1:5.) Unless watched and nurtured, the soul's health decays. Everything around us tends to injure the plants of grace. Just as a diligent study of God's word and a diligent companionship with sincere Christians are necessary to the purity and fulness of the Christ-life within, so a diligent prayer-communion with God is the essential condition of the spirit-life in us. There is an analogy here with the nerve-life of the body and its mysterious connections with magnetism, electricity, and other imponderable agents. Prayer takes this mysterious and powerful place in the soul's life, and diligence in prayer must accompany diligence in the word and Christian intercourse if we would have the whole spiritual man healthy and strong. Christ and the Holy Ghost are both indwellers of the believer; the entire spiritual life is in their presence and work. The word and communion with the saints nourish the Christ-experience, while prayer nourishes the Spirit-experience, and yet both are really one. As we have before seen, the two streams are for ever intermingling. One cannot take this Bible view of salvation and renewal without seeing that no natural growth could ever develop a Christian or a saint. There must be a new birth or a new begetting of God. And not only must the unconverted soul be made to realize this foundation fact, but the believer must ever renew its freshness in him, so that he may be saved sad legalistic and self-righteous mistakes in attempting to increase in holiness. Your growth, my Christian brother, is from within, not from without. It is only through God in you that you can grow. There is the root and sap of your spiritual life. Laws and rules and churches and ordinances have nothing to do with it, except as they are the products of it. A due thought of this will send you for a renewal of soundness and health, not to any form of external duty, but to your Bible and your knees. You will keep your *heart* with all diligence, as appreciating the truth that out of *it* are the issues of life. You will be jealous over it with a godly jealousy, and remember that it belongs to God. You will be to the world—that distinctive thing which belongs only to Satan—as one dead, and your life will be hid with Christ in God.

If you were sound in faith, healthy in your piety, what an impassable gulf would lie between you and the Christless world! **for God dwelleth in you!**

## CHAPTER III.

### THE SOUL'S FOOD.

"THY LAW DO I LOVE." Ps. 119:163.

IN the former chapters we have followed the analogy of the bodily life and spiritual life as suggested by Scripture, and have noted that as the blood-system and nerve-system mutually sustain one another, and the two form the sources of physical life, so the Lord Jesus Christ and the Holy Spirit in mysterious conjunction form the life eternal of the soul; and we have also noted that as the blood and nerve-fluid are furnished to the body through the food, so the indwelling of Christ and the Spirit is through the word of God; and, moreover, that as the blood and nerve-fluid thus originating are maintained in purity by means of the breath, exercise, and nervous influences, so the indwelling of Christ and the Spirit is made efficient by Christian communion, activity, and prayer. We have thus all the data from which to examine in detail the conditions of a healthy piety.

1. Our first consideration will concern the relation of the Christian to the *written word of God.* I use the word "written" advisedly, for to some minds it may appear arbitrary to bind a man's salvation to a book, which might be lost or put out of reach or become corrupted. Indeed, this is a very favorite objection to Christianity on the part of a large class of philosophers. They plead against it its injustice and partiality, as it makes salvation easier to some than to others; perhaps, indeed, impossible to many. No doubt there are sincere minds that struggle with this perplexity, and are inclined to feel that a revelation that is to all alike is the only revelation which they can accept, and that hence a written revelation they must reject. There is an apparent force in this argument, but yet a few moments'

thought will destroy it; for, in the first place, a revelation comes with its own proofs. Having thus proved itself, no outside considerations can invalidate it. Christianity is a revelation proved by its own inherent perfections and by the overwhelming evidences of the miraculous works attending its proclamation. From Genesis to Revelation, from Adam to John, its light shines in unmixed brilliancy, (for it is alike Christianity before and after the earthly life of Christ.) The divinity of the record is as clear to the unprejudiced mind as the celestial origin of the midday sun. God's grace raising man from sin to holiness through the sufferings of the God-man is a doctrine of grandeur and perfection that no human mind could ever have conceived; and all the accordant teachings of purity in the heart, love to God and man and renunciation of self, are both incomprehensible and repugnant to the natural man. Besides this heavenly aspect of the word, we have the external wonders wrought in its confirmation by Moses, Elijah and Elisha, and Christ and his apostles, done in no corner, but performed openly before nations, and deeply and permanently inscribed on the common memories and traditions of the race, as well as minutely recorded on the sacred pages. These testimonies do not wax weak through age, as some would falsely and craftily argue. Is a father's testimony to his early home any the less strong because the child has never seen that home, and never saw his father's childhood? When that child is himself a grandfather, is his testimony to his father's home any weaker to *his* grandchildren? It is a false formula that evidence grows weak by age. The character of the bearers, and not the time through which they bear it, can alone invalidate evidence. The miracles of Jesus and his apostles are just as potent testimonies to-day as they were when they were performed. Nobody can impeach the witnesses. The fulness of historic light shines on them, and they stand out as conspicuously as the Alps in the sunshine. False miracles and fabulous legends cannot bear investigation, but the miracles of Christ and the apostles court and rejoice in the most searching scrutiny. The more you compare the diamond and its imitation, the better for the diamond. He is a fool who, because of the imitation, flings all away and denies the diamond.

The written revelation coming thus to us with its attendant testimony within and without, it is the part of common sense to meet theoretical objections with contempt. When once a truth is established, we can occupy it as an impregnable fortress. This is the course of every right mind with the Scriptures. Having received their own abundant testimony, it consents to leave outside problems unsolved rather than stultify itself by denying the true Scripture for their solution.

But, secondly, the difficulty about the injustice of a written revelation may itself not appear so great, if we remember that the written word does not deny the spoken word, but is its preservation. The spoken word to Adam and Noah was to the whole race, and it is not for us to say how much of that spoken word has remained in tradition or thought or mental structure in the various nations of the earth. But to *us* the *written* word is *the* word, and hence we emphasize the adjective, and protest against any naturalism that would make all alike by destroying the Bible. "God in nature" is a favorite expression with souls that hate to think of sin and punishment, of penitence and pardon, of grace and gratitude. But "God in nature" is no comfort or help to the helpless spirit. The whirlwind, the earthquake, the storm, the overwhelming waves, the monsters of the sea and forest, the volcanic fires, the consuming thunderbolt, the desolating pestilence, the tortures of disease—these are some of the sweet comforts to the needy and sinking soul that "God in nature" presents. What right has the natural religionist to call out from nature some of its fair scenes and construct a revelation and a creed from this fragmentary eclecticism? If God is in nature as our instructor, he is instructor in *all* nature and not in part. If God's revelation to the help-seeking soul is through the workings of the physical system—the material creation—then common sense protests against any elimination in the record. If the naturalist point to the flower and the bird-song, to the winding brook and the frisking lamb, and exclaim as commentary on this text, "God is love—God is my Father," I have a right to point to the drought and the famine, to the deadly cobra's fang and the poisonous breath of the cholera, and exclaim as commentary on *this* text, "God is angry—God is my enemy." I defy any one to find a flaw in my reasoning. We have had so much of this sentimental naturalism, that it has obtained a circulation as of true coin, and sensible people are caught by its sophistries. Some of the blessed truths of God's word are attributed to nature as their author, when nature's voice is as dumb as the grave on these sublime themes; and then when nature is arrayed in these jewels from God's word, that word is rejected and cast out as a pretender. What does nature teach at the grave but corruption? What does she teach in sickness but decay? What does she teach in sorrow but despair? And this nature is the comforter, poor soul, to which you would flee in the day of your calamity!

It is something above and against nature that we need; something that shall say, "Thus far and no farther shalt thou go, and here shall thy proud waves be stayed;" something that shall rebuke the fever and the pain, as well as the winds and the waves; something that shall go deeper than pain and sorrow, to sin, the cause of all, and there apply a balm; something that shall give a triumph to the spirit in the face of conscience and the truth, and shall fill the heart with holy boldness. Before these requirements how nature shrinks away! "The depth saith, 'It is not in me,' and the sea saith, 'It is not in me.'" In the midst of nature's fairest garden we must look for the *Kol Jehovah*, the voice of the Lord God, as something very different from the trees, and which alone can touch the centre of our moral being and guide our feet in truth. That *Kol Jehovah* has never been wanting since sin rendered man helpless; and whatever speculation we may have regarding its character and method amid the wilds of barbarism or the refinements of elegant paganism, the practical fact for us is its presence with us in the Bible.

The ready suggestion of superficial skeptics,

that others have *their* Bibles as good as ours, and that it is vain for us to ignore the holy books of India, Persia, China and Arabia, is a suggestion quite like that of the naturalist for both its plausibility and its weakness. It is a very captivating liberality, apparently, that appeals to a young heart, and on the score of common justice bids it honor Vedas, Koran, and Bible alike. The same excellent liberality would have us honor Gaudama, Mohammed, and Jesus Christ alike; and a perfectly analogous and comprehensive liberality would call for an equal homage toward God and the Devil. "Good Lord, good Devil," would be the appropriate exordium to every prayer. It is no compliment to truth to spread its garments over error. It is no compliment to truth to represent her as looking any way and all ways. It is no compliment to truth to say "2 and 2 make 4 or 5 or 6, just as you please. We must be liberal and let each be true." If this be liberality, I know of no place so free as hell, where consistency is not a qualification for admission. If the Vedas are true, then the Koran and the Bible are lies; if the Koran is true, then the Vedas and the Bible are lies; and if the Bible is true, the Vedas and the Koran are lies. A pagan who honors the Vedas, or a Mohammedan who honors the Koran, is far more of a man than the so-called Christian, who pretends to honor Vedas, Koran, and Bible all alike. They are false, but he is both false and shallow. One reading of the Vedas or Koran will stop any sane man from comparing the Bible with them; and the Persian and Chinese books may be treated in the same way. Let me see the man who has read both and is in doubt which is the true, they or the Bible, and I 'll show you a man who has seen the sun and a tallow-candle light, and cannot for the life of him tell which is the perennial luminary. It is a reproach to humanity that such rubbish ever has to be cleared away before discussing the wonders of the Book of God. But the devil is never weary of putting the fool's cap on men.

The *Kol Jehovah*, the voice of the Lord God, is to us only in the Book of God. There are promptings and guidings in Providence and spiritual influences, but the *voice*, the articulated words and sentences that form the vehicle of organic truth — this divine defining utterance is found only in the Bible. The 119th Psalm, in the very centre of the Bible, is an enlargement on this great truth. In that psalm the psalmist uses seven different words to express the *written* revelation of God. He seems purposely to shut out any twisting of his words into a praise of "sermons in stones and books in the running brooks," and to confine the mind to the contemplation of that specific revelation which to-day we call, with its divine increase, the Bible. We cannot conceive of any other way in which God could have made his voice heard by the mass of mankind than by a written word. A literal voice, an appeal to the ear, would have reached the treatment of a natural phenomenon very shortly. It would have been put away from the conscience and soul with volcanoes and earthquakes; criticism would have erected its batteries, and thrown the shell of fixed law and subjective imagination into the whole system, or else the ear, accustomed to the sound, would have given it no heed. Moreover, the literal voice could not be examined, analyzed, and weighed, as can the written word and its potent evidences thus accumulated. It would have had to become a written word in order to dwell upon earth and be thoroughly known. And once a written word among men, there is a dishonoring of that word and a ruinous indulgence of man's sloth and neglect if a voice should be added to the revelation.

The written word is thus the light of our path. It is the perpetuation of heavenly truth, a candle lighted from the throne of God, which can never be extinguished. In its relation to the Christian, or the Christian's relation to it,

*It should be the "man of his counsel."*

This is the Bible phrase. In this very 119th Psalm we have the words, "thy testimonies are my counsellors," literally, "men of my counsel." This phrase of David corresponds to the words of Stephen, Paul, and Peter, who call the Scriptures the oracles or oracle of God. They are the ever-present source of instruction to the soul; and, as divine, can never fail to meet every want proposed. The fulness of God is found in his word, and this word is no more defective in its instruction than God is defective in his love and mercy. Hence, just as the ship's pilot is always at the helm with his eye upon the compass, so the healthy believer will be found ever directing his course by this unerring guide. This implies an intimate acquaintance with God's word that I am sure is not common. It implies the meditating in God's law day and night, which seems a mere Utopian expression to most Christians. But yet who wants a counsellor with whom he is not intimate? And how can you get the counsellor's mind unless you sit down with him by the hour and question him and lead out his manifold instructions? Is there much of this done by Christians? I put it to the honest opinion of my readers. Is God's oracle consulted, is his word pondered, is this divine counsellor received into intimate communion by the so-called people of God? Are not Christians pleading constantly that they have no time to search the Scriptures? This is their response to the Master! But is it not often a fear lest the Scriptures would rebuke much of their daily conduct that keeps them away? They desire not its counsel. The "man of their counsel" is not the man whose counsel is agreeable. But what can be substituted? Our reason is sadly deficient. God is not going to guide us by dream or magic. He has not promised a miracle. The Spirit's movement is always *through the word.* With the word unconsulted, no man can expect the inspiration of the Spirit. "To the law and to the testimony" is the cry of God to the soul. There and there only are our orders and guarantees. There is a practical necromancy among Christians, by which they substitute guesses, chances and native cunning for the authority and teaching of God's word. They walk by the sparks of their own kindling rather than seek God's gracious sunlight. The main book on the merchant's desk, on the lady's table, in the child's school, should be the Bible. It would regulate the action of commerce, society, and education. It would protect men in trade from the temptations to fraud and deceit, as well as from over-absorption in material interests; it would protect society from immodesty, extravagance, frivolity, and selfishness; and it would save the growing minds of the young from the poison of worldliness and practical infidelity, which form the staple of so many schools. Now, while this is the legitimate place and office of God's word as the man of our counsel, the average Christian is actually startled by the proposition. The Bible among ledgers! The Bible in a drawing-room! The Bible to be read and taught and consulted in our fashionable schools! How absurd! And so with a sneer in place of an argument, God's holy word is dismissed from the places where above all others it should appear as the "man of counsel;" and you may be sure that the hearts that have been ashamed of God's oracle in business and society will not be forward to consult it in the closet. The Bible is what we need to reform both business and society. To reinstate God's pure word in our haunts of commerce and our social gatherings, as the counsellor and thus the controller of all, should be the aim of every evangelizing spirit. Let the Christian, wherever he goes, be known as the Bible-man, the man who keeps this divine light over before his feet. For God to give the light and man to put it away from him is to court disaster and defy God. Alas! how many are doing that! How many are putting the divine counsellor into a dungeon (like Jeremiah) because he counsels things unpleasant to our greed or our low ambition?

Let us emancipate the Bible, and place it in its high position of immediate and perpetual counsellor to the soul, a position to which God has assigned it.

## CHAPTER IV.

### THE SOUL'S FOOD: LOVE FOR GOD'S WORD.

THE inspired word must be to the believer the *object of affection*.

Every path that leads to heaven is trodden by willing feet. No one is ever driven to Paradise. The very essence of a holy life, in its initiation and its consummation, is in the renewed will. It is a very gross view of heaven that counts it a place only, into which a man might be cast, whether he will or no. All true religion is a willing religion. Now the root of the will is in the affections. It is the new heart that makes the new life. A man wills to follow the truth, because he loves the truth. That new affection is the original germ of his godliness. And just as the Christian life is a willing life growing out of the affections, so every contribution to that life from God's grace is to be received into the love of the soul, before it can be made efficient. The Bible, God's revealed truth, is to be not only the soul's food, but the soul's *delicious* food, or else it does not at all adapt itself to the whole economy of God's salvation. God has no more prepared a bitter food for the soul, than he has prepared a painful heaven. The love that saves does not delight in tormenting. The unpalatableness of God's wine must be in the diseased palate. It is a favorite notion with some that God delights in making his people uncomfortable. They seem to think that Christ's sufferings for sin were not enough, but we must supplement them. Hence the way to heaven must be studiously beset with thorns in order to be orthodox. Reading Scripture as a penance belongs to this strange school of self-righteous piety. Under this pernicious infatuation, children are made to read portions of the Bible as utterly unmeaning to them as a page of the Integral

Calculus, and so a distaste and disgust for the Word of God is generated in their minds, and they grow up with an aversion to the Blessed Book as wholly unnecessary as a repugnance to their own mother. We must go back to first principles. If the means of grace are not delightful to us, it is our fault and not God's. If we wander away from God, he may send afflictions to awaken our conviction, but to suppose that he will regularly deal out to us affliction as our meat and drink, that he will give us a nauseous drug as our daily food, is insulting to the character of our Heavenly Father, and to the finished work of our Lord Jesus Christ. And yet to such a conclusion must we come, if we are to read the Bible only as a duty, if we are to take it up as a last resort, if we are to view it as a Romanist views his knotted cord, with which at appropriate times he must scourge himself. And is not this the prevailing notion in the church of Christ? At least, does not practice suggest the thought?

That the Bible should be disliked and avoided by unbelievers, whose unrenewed hearts would be ever rebuked by it, and whose unrenewed tastes would have no appreciation of its divine beauty, is by no means strange; but that the children of God, born into the kingdom of Christ and receiving the Holy Ghost, should have no other connection with the Word but that which conscience sternly compels, is a paradox which might make angels weep. Go through the families you know, and see this strange and sad phenomenon. In how many Christian families the Bible stands no chance with Shakespeare or the last novel! Rarely touched on a week-day, on Sundays even the biography or religious (?) newspaper is preferred to it. Love for the Bible! why, it is as rare as love for the prayer-meeting, and love for Christian communion. All these signs of spiritual health fail together. The fact of this apathy toward God's Word ought to alarm, but habit weaves its screen before the mind and it fails to see the dangers of its position. It was lately said that it would be a good thing to have an *auto da fé* now and then in every Christian community. An old-fashioned persecution might arouse the church of Christ and separate it from the world. And so a personal disaster might almost be sought in order to teach us the inestimable preciousness of God's Word. There is so much trifling in Christian circles, so much flitting hither and thither in chase of bubbles, so much superficial piety, so much zeal for ribbons, that unless disaster come and shake the earthly foundations, it seems impossible that deep and grand and heavenly thoughts can enter these souls and so the blessed Bible become a cherished treasure. I have read of a poor blind girl in France who obtained the gospel of Mark in raised letters, and learned to read it by the ends of her fingers. By the peculiar character of her daily toil her fingers became callous, and her sense of touch diminished till she could not distinguish the letters. One day she cut the skin from the ends of her fingers to increase their sensibility, only, however, to destroy it. She felt that she must now give up her beloved book, and weeping, pressed it to her lips, saying, "Farewell, farewell, sweet word of my Heavenly Father, food for my soul! I must part with thee!" But to her surprise, her lips, more delicate than her fingers, discerned the form of the letters. She read "Gospel according to Mark." Her soul, overflowing with gratitude, pours out thanks before the throne of her Father in heaven. All night she perused with her lips the holy book, and her heart overflowed with joy at the new acquisition.

Oh for such a love for God's word in the hearts of God's people! Shall we wait for disasters before we know our privileges and cultivate our true delights? Does it not seem sometimes as if we should have to become blind, so as not to see the glittering follies about us, in order to prize aright our Jesus and his Word? Are we not sometimes assured in our reflections that afflictive dispensations are a necessity for our promotion, that only the sternness of this treatment can transfer us to our true position and spiritual relations as the children of God? Nay, is not this the philosophy that unlocks the whole mystery of affliction? And to one who understands this philosophy may not many a blow be avoided by learning the lesson from those already received and flying to the refuge of Christ's bosom where peace is found? In urging Christians to love the Word, I am really urging them to love the Lord more. When they are filled with his love, they will love his love-letters. When they feel that no love-relation is so grand and so absorbing as that which binds them to the Saviour, they will then feel that no words are so sweet as his, no book so precious as that which speaks of him and speaks from him to the saved soul. And so, conversely, if the Bible is not lovingly pondered, then there is but little force in the love for Jesus, the appreciation of his glorious presence is dull, the thoughts of his wooing and winning work for the soul are benumbed.

And here let me call attention to a type of Christian often found, in which self-deception surrounds itself with plausibility. It is where the love of Christ is deemed sufficient without the Word. The Bible is neglected, and the soul comforts itself with knowing that it can commune with the Lord without any medium. While this is literally true, yet the danger is very great that where the argument is used, there is a substitution of nature, or vague sentiment, or art-dreams for Christ. If we stay long from the Bible where Christ's picture is, we are apt to form another sort of Christ in the soul, and a very carnal one, too. Many a professed Christian can consort fully with the world, separate himself from God's people, aud count the Bible stupid, and yet carry with him a supposed Christ. There is no security except in the ever fresh recurrence to the revealed Word. There is the likeness of the ineffable One. "They are they," says Jesus, "which testify of me." The Christ in the waterfall or meadow, the Christ in the marble or on the canvas, the Christ in the æsthetic transports of the mind, the Christ in the softness of a social refinement may be a mere spectacular Christ of the imagination, a low, human Christ, and not the divine Jesus who saves his people from their sins, who creates them anew, who expels from their hearts the love of the world by filling those hearts with himself, who sanctifies their motives, aims, and principles, and in short in their entire lives substitute God for self. As we have seen, the Christ who is in us is introduced within us by the word. Just as the blood of the body is formed from the food of the body, so Christ, the blood of the soul, is formed from the word, the food of the soul. The written word becomes the personal Word within us. A Christ without the Bible is as impossible as a salvation without a Christ. Neglecters of the Bible are neglecters of Christ, however much they may beguile themselves with some sentimental illusion, a pseudo-Christ in a pseudo-Christianity. The face of Jesus is so full of graces and glories that we cannot imagine it independently; we must *look upon* it to know it, and in the Bible only do we look upon it. There it is—that wonderful face of love and truth. The study of that face can never weary, the knowledge of its infinite beauty can never be complete. To go away from the Bible is to cloud over those features and introduce a distorting medium. Hence arise coldness, formalism, worldliness, and the anti-christ of religious dreaminess, which so many take in place of the Crucified.

These considerations make it evident that a love of God's word is a requisite for the true Christ-life of the soul. There will be, there *can* be no true application to that word except by love, and there can be no love for that word except where there is love of Christ, of whom that word is the exponent. The two are correlated and reciprocal. The love of Christ brings us to the Bible. The love of the Bible brings us to Christ. The two are indissolubly united in the very nature of truth. Woe to the soul that attempts their dissev-erance!

If any one, in the light of these truths, declares his desire to love the word, as he appreciates his dereliction in the past, and asks for counsel, as he feels it a hard thing to love what he does *not* love, the answer is found in the same light which prompts the question. Your whole religious life is out of sorts, if you do not love God's word. You need a revolution in your life. You have habits to be mended, ways to be abandoned, duties to be assumed, for your present sys-tem of life is not formed after Christ and his word. You are to draw nearer to Jesus in a love-consecration, and that with his word in your hands; and as in doing this, you feel that many a darling folly is slipping from your grasp, let them go. The love of Jesus will not bear such silly rivals. As Jesus becomes more known, the Bible will be more prized, and as the Bible is more prized, Jesus will become more precious and powerful to you. It is the two, then, you are to seek. Not Jesus without the Bible—that would land you in sentimentalism. Not the Bible without Jesus—that would make you a legal formalist. But the Bible and Jesus together; and drive everything out of your path that would interfere with your seeking.

If such a love of the word of God were rife in the church of Christ, we should see every Christian as eager to gain time for Bible meditation as he is to procure the morning paper. The desire would be before the sense of duty. As a consequence of this, he would *know* the Bible, its promises and precepts not only, but all its connections and inter-dependencies. More than that, the deep inner meanings of the word would be ever bubbling up to him like the diamond waters of a mountain spring, refreshing his whole being, and making him forget the weariness and toil of life. He would become, as it were, inspired by the divine truth. It would be so interwoven into his nature, that its heavenly principles would not have to be sought after, but would spontaneously assert themselves in all his movements.

The perplexed questions of duty would all disappear before the tutored promptings of a Bible-pervaded soul. Casuistry would have no place where God's philosophy would rule. The life, surcharged with truth would, besides, electrify all its contacts with truth's power. If the church would thus feed earnestly and heartily on God's word, its whole tone of action and conversation would be marvellously changed. It would be taking the divine means of elevation to an angelic standard. The ordinary themes of material life would shrink to their subordinate position and the busy nothings which consume so much time and thought would be lost in the substantial occupations of a healthy piety. Such power has the Bible and the Bible only. Such transmutations of the whole man can it alone produce, for it is the wisdom of God and the power of God in the receptive heart. Oh! it is this power we need amid the mass of frivolity that encumbers the church, and makes it drag on its way so awkwardly and slowly towards the millennium. Millennium! can it be that God's people are seeking and longing for its glories? Is its sheen of beauty a captivating prospect to their faith? Is its peace and holiness a star of guidance to their pilgrim feet? Nay, rather, are not ceiled houses and ephemeral comforts or displays contenting their thoughts and aspirations, and God's sweet coming dawn forgotten in the artificial lights of the present night-time? And is it not all this wrong arrangement of our Christian life that is making its most natural mistakes in our view of everything else? Does not it give death the very name as well as character which it has no right to in a Christian's mind? Does not it emphasize every loss and disappointment with a tone of anguish, where each should be arrayed with a crown of hope? Does not it tarnish all the gold of love with the rust of selfishness? Oh for faith in God's Bible, a faith that would work by love and gather daily the manna, lifting the thankful eye to the gracious heaven that sent it! This is the angels' food. It is only they who love Egyptian slavery who can loathe it. The angelic character will prize the angelic fare. I would that the testimony of the dying saint whose heart is all aglow with the life-touch of the word, of the poverty-stricken child of God who revels in the eternal wealth of the Scriptures, of the despised and rejected believer who in the holy lore has learned how to despise all human contumely and scorn, of the heart smitten down to death that has achieved a glad resurrection at the voice of the heavenly truth—I would that the testimony of these, mingling in one grand chord of celestial harmony, could be concentrated upon the souls of all who read this, and persuade them now to put themselves in full relation with the living oracles. It is as we listen to our God speaking, that the great God-life tingles through our souls; it is as we receive the sentiment and the logic of the skies that the dreariness and obscurity of earthly sentiment is lost, and the false and unsatisfying logic of the world is driven to its tomb. Walking with God is the summit of privilege and happiness, and that exalted walk is found when the voice of prayer and praise has birth and sustenance in the soothing voice of God speaking through the revealed word, to the listening and enraptured spirit. Here is the secret that so many miss. They turn hither and thither in unrest, while their Beloved is near them in vain. They do not know the talismanic power of this neglected Book. No enchanted carpet, that bore the fabled prince to wished-for realms, could so transfer the soul to the companionship of glory. All stories fail to reach the high analogy, and represent the rare discoveries of peace and spiritual plenty to which the trusting heart is borne by this celestial vehicle of grace, which wears so earthly and so unpretending form. Fear not to give yourselves to the love of the Bible. There can be no idolatry here. Idolatry can only cling to the letter, but it is the spiritual voice of the word to which the Lord invites us, when he says, "Search the Scriptures—for they are they which testify of *Me*." If you believe that that Lord Jesus is worth more than all besides, if you recognize your own salvation as his fond work, if you know that the all of God that can shine on human hearts resides in that blessed Christ, then leap to the happy task of learning that Saviour better by the means himself has provided. No longer let the Bible be a book respectfully neglected; no longer let its divine light reach you only through the imperfect media of human treatises or human lips; but press through, for the way is open to you, press through all interposing veils, and in the Holy of holies bathe your exultant spirit in the radiance that there overflows from the oracle of God.

# CHAPTER V.

## THE SOUL'S FRESH AIR.

"HE THAT WALKETH WITH WISE MEN SHALL BE WISE." PROV. 13 : 20.

"IT is not good for man to be alone" was God's own declaration at the birth of the race. A man's society is as necessary to his growth as his individuality. Indeed he has no individuality except in society. He is born with tendrils, and begins with life to grope for something to clasp. His thoughts are not his own till he has communicated them to others, and his moral sense is but a blunt potentiality till it is developed toward his fellows. The Church of God is founded on this principle. It is an aggregation, or congregation, with its infinite collateral supports. It is like the golden boards of the tabernacle standing together and bound together by golden bars, preserving the unity of the Spirit by the bonds of peace, and forming together a dwelling for the God of the church, in which an acceptable service is offered and where the light of His glory shines from between the cherubim. The "assembling of ourselves together" is a token of the social union of believers in Christ and a divine hint of this essential principle of Christian growth and health. Hermitages and monasteries are Buddhist, not Christian institutions, defying the revealed will of God and the spiritual instincts of the new birth. As the fresh air is necessary for the lungs, by which they perform their renewing functions, and purify the blood of the body, so the society of believers is necessary to the spiritual life, preserving it from a false entrance of the word and a false development of Christ in the soul. The word is the soul's food, but the society of God's people is the soul's inbreathing, and God has ordained the one as well as the other that Christ may be truly and fully formed in us as the healthy blood is formed in the body.

God's people to-day have to be instructed in this great truth, as the Corinthian Christians were instructed by Paul. The Corinthian Christians fell into the society of worldly people, the usual arguments of rank, position, wealth, fashion urging them to this course. The apostle traces their spiritual misfortunes to this sad error. He shows them that their social relations should be confined to believers; that between the soul with Christ and the soul without Christ a great gulf was fixed—blessed be God, not an impassable one, and hence courtesy, kindness, and compassionate interest might stretch across it, but yet it was a great gulf—which forbade the communion of intimacy and the confidential relations of the inner friendship. A bridging of this gulf was a betrayal of truth, an alliance with the enemy, a degradation of the holy standard, a reproach to Christ. Hear the apostle's words: "Be ye not unequally yoked together with unbelievers; for what fellowship hath righteousness with unrighteousness? or what communion hath light with darkness? and what concord hath Christ with Belial? or what part hath a believer with an unbeliever? ....... Wherefore come out from among them and be ye separate, saith the Lord, and touch not the unclean thing; and I will receive you and will be a Father unto you, and ye shall be my sons and daughters, saith the Lord Almighty." If all this does not refer to the social relations of Christians, to what else *can* it refer? That the Corinthians were idolaters does not help the matter, for while that fact *is* objected against them as one argument for separation from them, yet the main argument is that they were *unbelievers.* The apostle's argument and apostolic order are, therefore, for to-day as for then, for this nominally Christian land as for pagan Corinth. This ἑτεροζυγία or unequal yoking together is the social intimacy of believer with unbeliever. An idolater is no worse than any other unbeliever. The unbelief is what does the mischief in society. It steals unobserved into the Christian's heart from his contact with moral and excellent unbelievers, and the poison is more subtle as the unbeliever is more moral and high-minded. Christ is unthroned and a new Christ is introduced. The believer wishes to be on the same plane with his intimate friend, and so lowers his distinctive and specific truth to the level of some general religion, which is at bottom the substitution of a self-philosophy for revelation. In this way, hearts that have been enlightened by the Holy Spirit to behold the cross have given up both light and cross in order to perform the behests of a high-toned friendship. Beauty of sentiment and even philanthropy are used in cementing this "unequal yoking," against which it is perilous to argue, for noble sentiment and philanthropy are fine things and they demand recognition and homage from all; and so by these specious means the Christian is un-Christed and thrown into a wide and dreary sea of natural religion, the religion of birds, beasts, and fishes.

Another style of mind fares no better—in outward appearance, worse. In this case the believer by social communion with unbelievers who love and live for display, soon begins to form the same tastes and cultivate the same desires with them. The gay life is led, the spiritual promptings to a useful life are repressed even to paralysis, worldly excitement becomes the only food the soul can feed on, and the name of the holy Christ is dragged by the apostate believer into this career of mockery. Sometimes gross sins, such as those which even the world proscribes, yawn to engulf such a straying believer, putting a condemnation upon him in his own sight which he had long since had in the sight of the angels.

Another style of mind, by this unequal yoking, is found making moneyed gains by low and selfish ways, grinding the faces of the poor and taking advantage of others' misfortunes under the robber's plea, "all is fair in trade." By a close association with the unbelieving in the conduct of financial business, not only are the heavenly graces of forbearance, charity, and brotherly love quenched, but common justice is abused. Christians cheat one another under the name of business transactions; they accumulate riches by deceit and fraud; they leave debts unpaid while they indulge in luxurious living, taking advantage of some technicality of weak human law and forgetting the unalterable divine law; they bring up their children for the same feverish mammon-worship and plunge them into the same temptations with the specious plea, "Oh! all the world does it; we must not run counter to the current of life." Such are some of the manifold and fearful evils which arise for the Church of Christ from this ἑτεροζυγία or unequal yoking together of believers with unbelievers. Young and thoughtless Christians, without much experience, have very little idea of this truth, and are ready to combat it with much indignation. "Is not the Gospel liberal? Does it not preach charity? and now am I to give up my intimacies with my sworn friends on the ground of a Gospel demand? That would be a narrow Puritanism—a wretched bigotry—I 'll do nothing of the kind. I *will* have friends who are not believers." And so the will, captivated by the world, makes its indignant decision, while the Holy Spirit speaks in vain with warning voice, "What part hath a believer with an unbeliever?" The love of holy things steals away so imperceptibly—the love of worldly things steals *in* so imperceptibly—the whole transmutation is so very natural, without jar or surprise, that the young Christian does not realize the dreadful change. The young man must go into business, but he forgets that it is his Christian duty to discriminate in business; and the young woman must go into society, but she forgets that it is her Christian duty to discriminate in society. Neither into business nor society have I a right to go, except by the Lord's own ways. If I do otherwise, I lose all the Lord's privileges. And to go into either of them through worldly intimacies is to despise the Lord's way altogether.

"But oh! how much I should have to give up!" says the young Christian, thinking of worldly successes, worldly applause, the gains of avarice or vanity. Very well. Did you never hear Jesus say anything about plucking out a right eye and cutting off a right hand for him? This is the very eye he wishes you to pluck out—the very hand he wishes you to cut off. It will save your soul. This worldly society is sapping your spiritual vitality. You are too young to know the full force of the truth. Take older Christians' word for it. Take Christ's word for it: "What part hath a believer with an unbeliever?"

And now let us look at the positive side of this question. Let us ask how a believer *is to form* his social alliances, since we have seen how he is *not* to form them.

In general he is to select godly souls for his intimates. The divine word enunciates the universal principle: "He that walketh with wise men shall be wise." The wisdom of which God's word treats is the wisdom which practically recognizes the claims of God on the heart and life, and the wise man is the godly man. The first meaning of that passage in its high sense is, that *godliness is promoted by communion with the godly;* and the next inferential meaning is, that *the proper communion of the godly is with the godly.* We need not stop here to examine the psychological principle on which these truths are founded. Personal esteem, desire to please, self-approval, unconscious imitation, the necessities of social combination—all these are elements of the working by which like begets like, by which social life is a crucible of assimilation. But more than assimilation is obtained. There is augmentation—increase of force for good or for evil, in the alliances of society. "As iron sharpeneth iron, so a man sharpeneth the countenance of his friend." The old adage is universally received, "In union is strength." Social union strengthens all the distinctive features of the union. Is it a worldly society? The worldliness is intensified and raised to a higher power by the union. Is it a godly society? The spiritual truth and beauty of the alliance are enhanced by the very fact of the communion.

In putting then the general principle into practice, there is, first, the duty of Christian parents to select the early companions of their children with care, and exclude the vicious and evil-disposed, even at the cost of sundering friendships and alienating relatives. Better, far better to say farewell for ever to the parents, however dear, than to ruin your offspring for ever by the contaminating influence of the ill-trained and sin-indulged children. Then, in riper years, when your children have understood their relation to God as redeemed by the blood of Christ—and the children of all Christians should early reach that understanding and personal faith—it is for you to bestow much supervision upon the friendships that are formed in the tender and heedless days of youth. You have the power to invite to your house the proper young friends and to keep out the improper. Exercise this power as to God. Let no laws of etiquette set aside the law of God. If you have to cut off whole families of the highest respectability and most desirable position from your circle, by refusing special home-friendships to their young people, cut them off with the independence of an emperor. Let the dukes and marquises go, and good riddance to them, that your children may escape the pollution of the vain life with which their worldly children would inoculate them. Never let your children have the beginning of these low but fascinating tastes. It is the little beginning that whets the appetite for more, and then the indulgent parent begins to say, "How can I keep my dear children from society?" by "society" meaning simply this gay and worldly form of society; and this cry of the parent is a response to the cry of the child who has tasted the glittering vanity, "How could you coop me up and make my life to languish by imprisonment?" where the dreadful imprisonment and the cruel treatment, suggestive of the Tower of London and Smithfield, are only the withholding of the child from the poison of a fashionable or semi-fashionable life. If you would only begin at the beginning with your children, you would avoid all trouble on this score. Alas! too often you think far less of their souls' health and God's will than of earthly preferment for them and yourselves, and so you are drawn in, and they too, and sink in the vortex.

But, secondly, turning from parents, I speak to young Christians themselves, and urge them to ally themselves with one another. Do not say that Christians are too few. How many intimate friends do you want? Six or eight are as many as one person can well manage.

Two or three are a more available number. Can you not find six or eight Christian friends, who in taste and education and refinement suit you? Did you ever try? Did you ever ask God to help you find them? The trouble, I think, has been in your utter carelessness in the matter. You have never felt it to be an important question. You must feel the truth from God, and then you will find the way to conform to it.

The social side of our nature is not developed, as it should be, in our churches. There is a repellant coldness that is unseemly and un-Christian. All the childish folly of caste and rank which belongs to the world as one of its bawbles is assumed by the Church of Jesus, which ought to live above it and despise it. Tosses of the head, supercilious airs, "I 'm better than you" looks, which are very suitable to an ignorant world that has no God, are found among those who have been exalted to be the brothers and sisters of the Lord of glory. No denunciation of all this can be too strong. The church must make the breach between it and the world wider, must cut off all communications except those of courtesy and Christian help, must live within itself and thus nourish the Christ-life, and in its own work among the poor, the ignorant, and the young must make and cement the social union of its own members. What a strange idea inhabits some Christian minds, that young Christians can only be happy when allowed to mingle with worldly people! Society with Christian companions cannot produce happiness! There is the same lamentable notion of divine things in such thinkers as in the boy who asked his father, "Father, when I get to heaven, if I am real good, wont God let me come down here on Saturdays and play?" What a dreadful notion of heaven that boy had! And what a dreadful notion of Christianity and Christians must that mind have that thinks a happy life on earth must be spent in worldly associations! The Church of Jesus has within it all the elements of social happiness. It is our fault if we do not utilize them. The social evening, that centres around a Scripture reading, or that ends with the worship of the Heavenly Father, who gives us the social happiness, is only distasteful to the heart that has been weaned away from God by the seductions of a godless society. The sweetest and tenderest relations of social life would be nurtured in such an atmosphere, instead of the formal, selfish, jealous, hypocritical excitements which have so largely usurped and monopolized the name of society. The recreation of such reunions would promote the vigor of health in body and soul, and fit every one for his or her appropriate duties of the family and home, instead of making those duties insipid and onerous, and causing them to be slighted as is done by the feverish nervousness generated in the false social ways of the world. Family divisions would be avoided, and all that dreariness which marks so many Christian households would be wanting. The family ties strengthened would preserve the young from the attractions of outside and questionable amusements which now lure millions to their ruin. Does the question arise in any mind, "How can I, already entangled in this net of evil, extricate myself? I am now fully committed to this false society.

I have my worldly intimacies and all the engagements which they naturally demand. It were comparatively easy for one beginning life and free from these embarrassments to select a Christful circle of associates and friends, but how can I?" The reply is, "You are to *cultivate a taste you have vitiated.*" That requires determination and prayerful attention. Moreover, in all the ways your judgment (not your taste) suggests, you are to withdraw from your mistaken alliances, substituting for them those that God will approve, and in this way help to reform your taste. In short, you have a work to do. The change will not come like the opening of a flower or the fall of a leaf, but your higher powers must do what your higher sense recognizes to be God's will. In such a work the Holy Spirit will be with you and give you success in the end and joy in the way.

"He that walketh with wise men shall be wise." The world's people are not wise, and God's people ought to know it. Wisdom has its criterion just beyond the grave. By that let us be ready to be tested. Let us be as singular as need be, if only with our Lord Jesus himself it can be said of us, "Wisdom is justified of her children." The company we keep is an index of the heaven we seek. Do we expect the association of the wise hereafter? We shall form their alliance now.

As we said at the outset, Christ is formed healthily and fully in him alone who breathes the air of Christian intercourse.

# CHAPTER VI.

## THE SOUL'S EXERCISE: IN THE FAMILY.

"EXERCISE THYSELF UNTO GODLINESS: FOR BODILY EXERCISE* PROFITETH LITTLE, BUT GODLINESS IS PROFITABLE UNTO ALL THINGS, HAVING PROMISE OF THE LIFE THAT NOW IS AND OF THAT WHICH IS TO COME." 1 TIM. 4:7, 8.

THERE may be to the Christian a regular feeding upon God's word and also a true communion with God's people, and so Christ be formed in him daily, while yet there may be a great deficiency in his spiritual life. Remember the figure. The body may feed on healthy

* I take Chrysostom's and De Wette's view of *σωματικὴ γυμνασία.*

food and breathe a healthy air, but unless it exercise itself in this air, the assimilation will be imperfect and the secretions irregular. So there must be an exercise of the spiritual man, an experimental use of his graces, if the word is to profit him as it should. We have seen how that word should be the man of his counsel and be loved by him in that capacity, and we have seen how his intimacies should be formed among those who have like precious faith in Jesus with himself. Let us now note the necessity and character of that exercise of his gifts by which his true spiritual health is promoted.

Paul's entreaty to Timothy, which we have placed at the head of this chapter, is to "*exercise himself* unto godliness," to act in his Christian life as the athlete acts in his bodily training and development. It is (so to speak, with reference to the Greek word *gymnasia* used by Paul) a charge to Timothy to make constant use of spiritual gymnastics. The comparison is direct. Bodily exercise is a benefit, but only for a short time, (see margin,) but the exercise of the soul in its graces is for all time and eternity. The health of the soul is far more important than the health of the body; and all we do here to promote the health of the soul tells upon the soul's history for ever. This is the apostle's argument. Let us apply it.

I. In looking at the necessity of spiritual exercise, we draw from the body's analogy that exercise conduces to health by quickening the circulation, dissipating false accretions, and bringing into play the utmost corners of the respiratory organs. Putting this into a spiritual translation, we have this: that spiritual exercise conduces to spiritual health by making the presence of Christ more vividly and intensely felt, (for Christ is the blood of the soul,) by shaking off morbid views and prejudices, and by developing the social Christian life to the fullest degree, for the respiration of the Christian is in the atmosphere of Christian communion. We may add, that where these results follow this cause, there is also a grand, healthy appetite for the word, the food of the soul. But let us look at each detail a moment.

1. The exercise of our gifts conduces to spiritual health by making the presence of Christ more vividly and intensely felt and operative in the soul.

We all know how hearty exercise of the body makes the blood tingle to the very extremities with a glow of vigor. We feel the oneness of our frames by this self-assertion of the physical life in all its parts, a oneness of coöperation and harmony, and not a oneness of conflict and discord as that which pain might give. Just so, when a Christian takes an active part in the common Christian life and ministers to it with the free use of his gifts, the very needs of the exercise bring Christ uppermost to his thoughts. His dependence upon his Lord for strength and enlightenment is felt, and the sweet comforts of his Lord's help is his rich reward at every step. There is no such bliss to the soul this side heaven as the consciousness of the Redeemer's full presence. It is not the pleasure of a beautiful sentiment striking the æsthetic perception, nor is it the Archimedean delight of discovery before a new glimpse of intellectual truth, but it is the ineffable joy of a felt union with the living God, of the direct and all-supplying love of the divine Saviour. It is the realization toward the Maker and Ruler of all of the phrase which grace teaches faith, "I am my beloved's and my beloved is mine." It is beauty and truth not beheld, but lived. I know of no way to this high and holy realization but that of the exercise of our spiritual abilities as God has given them. Mere contemplation will not do it. That is apt to make dreamers and to deceive the soul with sentimentalities. It will develop self rather than Jesus. In the look, the word, the act *for* our Lord we forget self and receive the *joy* of the Lord.

2. The exercise of our gifts conduces to spiritual health by shaking off morbid views and prejudices. These tokens of spiritual disease come generally from the ignorance that attends on the *vis inertiæ* or sluggishness of the soul. The analogies of truth are not observed, the interlacings and practical modifications of doctrine are ignored, and hence some notion is cultivated at the expense of

others, and a Christian cheats himself into believing the redness of inflammation to be the glow of health and a morbid swelling to be the fulness of vigor. All sorts of queer and pernicious doctrines are tenaciously held—they may be either on the one hand in the service of asceticism, or on the other in the service of self-indulgence. The diseased symptoms appear in both directions, perhaps more commonly in the latter. Now, what the patient wants is simple exercise for Jesus—an activity of his spiritual functions—the use of Christian society not only to receive influences therefrom, but to bestow influences thereon; and when his soul is shaken in such exercise, as well as in positive action toward the unconverted, his sickly excrescences will be shaken off, and his Christian character become symmetrical and wholesome. The apostolic character is formed in apostolic occupation. The mere spiritual cultivation of self is the way to hinder true self-cultivation.

3. The exercise of our gifts conduces to spiritual health by developing the social Christian life to the fullest degree. The sympathies

are aroused from their depths, the profoundest recesses of our being are touched by the vivid realizations of Christian brotherhood, and the Christ-life of each is felt on each in heart-recognitions that are like the intercourse of heaven. We have noted the analogy in the deep inbreathing in bodily exercise by which the remotest lung-cell is distended and the life is in fullest motion and efficiency. Here is the glory of true Christian society, not the sepulchral formality which some exhibit, who make Christian society a conscience-task as over against the worldly society they revel in, but that which warm-hearted Christians enjoy as they perceive in each other (with all their faults) the lineaments of Jesus. It is this which gives an electric thrill to life and makes society a heavenly thing. The exercise of our spiritual gifts brings us inevitably into such a social experience. The sons of the prophets go in companies. If you speak to the unregenerate, you wish a kindred heart to beat with yours in the action; and if you contemplate the goodness of God in any of its aspects, you would have another heart made a connoisseur by grace to double your joy by joining you in the contemplation. Activity for the Lord will always bring you into close union with the people of the Lord.

Such, then, are the elements of the necessity of spiritual exercise for spiritual health. We proceed to detail,

II. The character of that exercise.

A mistake is very often made by earnest Christians in supposing that activity for Christ must always be in one of the more apparent forms of teaching a class or making missionary visits. Now these two forms must ever be paramount in the church's view. The teaching of God's word and the visitation of the destitute are specified in the Scriptures as potent and practicable forms of glorifying Christ's name. Wherever we have the opportunity to undertake these royal styles of Christian exercise, undoubtedly we should use it. The number we can influence in a class, and the sympathy we can show to the suffering, make these forms of Christian work preferable to all others. But Christian exercise has a far wider application. It is the positive exercise of every grace that tends God-ward or to complete godliness. The practice of forbearance, gentleness, meekness, self-restraint, and holy earnestness in the daily duties and occurrences of life, in the family, in the haunts of commerce, and in the offices of professional activity is itself a wholesome spiritual exercise. But there is much more to be done than this. Each sphere of life presents its own claims and opportunities.

1. Are you a parent? Then it is yours to provide systematically for the education of your children in the truth; and here is a field of Christian effort directly at hand, full of advantage to yourself as to others, and from which no possible excuse can exempt you. Conversation with your children upon vital truths of revelation with endeavors to bring out their active appreciation, prayer with them that will ever make most sacred the memory of your instructions and impress upon them the sense of God's presence in the family, regular instruction from God's word, so that they become familiar with the Bible as the book of the heart—these are the forms of

Christian exercise which God sets before you. To the mother especially do these home ministrations appertain. She is, or should be, always the careful executive of home. Her eye should watch all the details of the family and her direct influence should be hourly felt in every part of the household. As familiarly acquainted with all, and as looked to for counsel and direction by all, she should, as the Lord's representative, see that the Lord's truth is made known to her children and her servants. Many mothers find it no hardship to dress and adorn their daughters for balls, to initiate them into all the hollow cant of ball-rooms, receptions, matinées, and operas, and to accompany them into the frivolous excitements of the world, while they have no time or strength to teach them the word of God or to train them as disciples of Jesus. These Christian mothers bring many a woe to the Church of Christ. If they had no children, we might pass them by without emphasis, but through their children they are operating with formidable power upon future generations to degrade Christianity and defile the streams of truth. The true disciple of the Lord, finding herself at the head of a family, will use time and talent, first of all, to consecrate her household unto Him; and in doing this, she will find very soon that the demands of the gay, godless world must be flatly resisted. The difficulties that often occur with Christian mothers arise from a want of perception of this fact: that a training for the world and a training for Christ are incompatible; that this point-blank refusal to the world is an absolute necessity for the spirituality of the family. The mother sees all her acquaintances educating their daughters to be butterflies, and she must do the same. How can she make herself conspicuous by saying "No"? She must go with the multitude to do evil, rather than follow Christ. And so she wastes money, thought, and time on diamonds and dresses and hair-ornaments, and acts as Satan's agent to destroy her daughter's soul. Her conscience frequently rebukes her with neglect of her daughter's higher interests, but the rebuke is answered by a hypocritical sigh, "O dear me! this perplexing life! I have no time for anything!" Ah! tell the truth, Christian mother, tell the truth: "Plenty of time for the world; but no time for God!" You have acted as though you felt in your own heart that all real enjoyment was to be found in the excitements of the world, and so you have taught your daughter the same fearful falsehood, until religion in your house is a mockery, just the fag end of legalism and nothing more. The true disciple nips this mischief in the bud. She cuts off the world. She finds cheerfulness and joy and rational amusement in a truly Christian life. She does not have to go to unbelievers to ask how to be happy. By cutting off the world, she has both time and taste to teach her family the ways of God. By doing this, she has achieved an independence with all its peace that a million of dollars could not give.

A practical question comes up here. How are we to act toward servants of a false and bigoted faith? The answer is, to use discretion and prayer. We cannot rudely assault prejudices. We ought not to magnify points of difference. We ought not to excite suspicion.

We ought not to meddle with subordinate details of their creed or worship. But the mother of a family has a thousand opportunities tc say a word for Jesus to the servant attending her, without arousing any personal church-feeling. The duties of trusting the Saviour for his pardon and of seeking his Holy Spirit might be often urged without any distinctive polemic being exhibited.

Family prayer is a grand centre for household piety. The servants of a different faith may not appear, and they should never be forced; but the family proper should always be gathered at this holy service. And it should be made an honest, earnest, touching service. The prayer should be *felt* by the leader, who ought to be the father of the family, and the Scripture should be read with reverence and attention. Oh! how much influence for life goes forth from the family altar! The children carry the scene before their minds, of the family group and the father reading God's word, long after the father's body has crumbled into dust, and the meaning of that scene is a constant quickener to the conscience. The excuses for the neglect of family worship are all vain. Want of time, want of ability, tardiness of the family and interruption of visitors are the pleas most frequently used. They scarcely deserve a reply. *Make* time, as you would for eating. Use a written prayer, if you cannot make an extemporaneous one; insist, as father of your family, upon a punctual attendance of all the members, and invite your visitors to bow the knee with you. Never let an excuse find itself at home in your religion that you would thrust out of your business. Sunday may be made a high day of profit to your family. Gather your children about you on the holy day. Read together with them from the Word. Let them talk with you freely about what they read. Encourage their questions. Search with them for answers, if they are not at hand, and set *them* to searching. Children are soon delighted with this looking up truth. Then pray and sing with them; tell them stories of your own Christian experience and of God's good providence to you; talk to them of the works of God in nature and grace; read to them the narrative of some true life; explain some picture of Bible story; and so most cheerily and happily use the golden opportunity of the day of rest for your family's lasting benefit in the Lord. Remember that no Sunday-school can shoulder a parent's responsibility, nor can it wield a parent's power. The parent was commissioned and ordered of God to conduct the spiritual education of his children when God first founded and organized his church upon earth. "Thou shalt teach my words diligently unto thy children, and shalt talk of them when thou sittest in thy house, and when thou walkest by the way, and when thou liest down, and when thou risest up." That divine ordinance has never been abrogated. There is in it a principle that time never can destroy. Here, then, Christian parents, is one of the methods of the exercise of your spiritual gifts, in which your spiritual health is advanced. Are you engaged in it? Is the truth of God written upon the posts of your house and on your gates? Have sacred associations been planted by you in the fruitful soil of home, whose fruit shall refresh your children to all generations? If you have been remiss here, for the sake of your own spiritual health be remiss no longer. Rise up, as a servant of God, shake off lethargy and all excuses, cut off all associations that interfere, and make your home a temple of the Lord God of salvation. Go forward in mind to your last hour upon earth and take a view of all your excuses from that stand-point. See how trivial they appear. Then re-consecrate your family to the Lord. Rejoice in the spiritual work that this lays upon you. It will quicken your whole spiritual being, animate your faith, sharpen your appetite for the truth, and give your life a zest you never knew before. You will, moreover, in making your house a bethel, institute the strongest practical antidote against the world-poison that is spread through the atmosphere and which corrupts the very vitals of religion. You will be furnishing to your children, not an ephemeral pleasure which will at last disgust the soul that sought it, but an abiding joy in the consciousness of a family bound together by heavenly ties and dwelling for ever in the blessed light of God.

# CHAPTER VII.

## THE SOUL'S EXERCISE: IN CHURCH RELATIONS.

THE church of Christ has life and organization, and is thus prepared for growth. Its Author and Head expects it to grow. The Spirit's exhortations through the inspired apostles have this growth of the church their constant theme. Its continuance on earth is for the very purpose of growth. The only true solution of the postponement of judgment upon a guilty world is found in the increase of Christ's church, and the development of the divine seed. Now this growth of the church consists of two parts, the furtherance of grace in the converted soul, and the conquest of new souls by the same grace. By the former the church grows deeper, by the latter it grows broader.

To whom is this responsibility of growth confided? Have we any authority for selecting any body or class of men in the church and placing this distinctive duty in their hands? Is there any warrant in Scripture for counting the officers of the church (whatever name we may give them) as the exclusive agents of God in building up the spiritual Zion? The love of power on one hand, and the love of ease on the other, have confirmed this error, so that over a large part of nominal Christendom the fallacy is working, and its natural result is found in a ceremonial and formal church. The gospel idea of the church is that of a body, where every member has its appropriate function in building up the whole, where responsibility is equally shared by all, and the privileges of activity equally enjoyed by all. Diversity of gifts and hence diversity of operations are to be noted, but nowhere do we learn that there is to prevail a distinction of gifts and no gifts. The same Spirit, from whom comes every endowment, moves in all. The power to work for Christ is not in the natural faculties, but in the Spirit. The most imposing natural faculties are nothing without the Spirit, and the Spirit is powerful to accomplish the grandest results where the natural faculties are weak and contemptible. These truths, which are the very A B C of spiritual knowledge, have to be reiterated, when we are discussing the subject of Christian work, for faith seems ever to fail in accepting them, and the church is full of idlers because of the excuse of the lack of natural faculties.

We have already addressed heads of families and pointed out to them the golden opportunities God has set before them in the careful training of their children and households in the truth. We now take a wider range of remark, and call upon every Christian to do his part in the organization of believers which we call a particular church, that is, his part of the church universal. In this assembly of believers for praise, prayer, instruction, and mutual sympathy and edification, we see the fairest type of the heavenly society that can be found on earth. This concourse of saints is not only a banquet of divine love, but also in some sort what the Greeks called an "eranos" or feast to which each guest contributes something. It is first very clear that no one man can pray or praise for another. If one leads, all should follow audibly or inaudibly as the case may be; but surely there is no worship where there is no following. A listless demeanor or intermittent attention, as if a Christian were at a spectacle, is a complete breach of divine order and a prostitution of the sacred occasion. We may expect the world to exhibit such conduct in the assembly, but where is the believer's heart that he should imitate the world in this his high place of privilege? The same course of thought holds good with regard to the instruction given by those appointed to the work. No Christian has a right to go to hear merely a pleasant speech, to make eloquence the object of his search, in going to the congregation of the saints. There is fearful remissness and injurious error here. Christians are seeking sensation, excitement, amusement, when the one thing to be sought is instruction from God's word. If that is not given, a Christian has a right to complain; but when that is given, it is every believer's duty to listen reverently not to man but to God, and so receive the divine seed into a good and honest heart.

There is another exercise in the assembly in which every Christian should engage. Giving is worship. Jehoiada placed the chest for offerings next to the altar of sacrifice. The apostle ordered collections to be made for the poor on the Lord's day. The giving to the Lord of our substance has always been, from the beginning of the church, an act of worship and a means of grace. No Christian has a right to except this from his worship. If a widow whose whole fortune was two mites, which made together one farthing, was by our Saviour commended for her pecuniary gift to the Lord's cause, who is there that can reasonably excuse himself on the ground of poverty? Christian men worth thousands and hundreds of thousands contract their whole souls into mean proportions, and rob themselves of large enjoyment in the divine life by putting their ten cents into the plate, while the poor excuse themselves altogether from giving. All this is wrong. The pecuniary gifts of God's people ought to be multiplied by a hundred, and then the giving church would be richer and happier for its gifts. Every one should give, whether rich or poor. The cent of the straitened is as much needed for worship as the dollar of the richer. The poor man should no more omit giving because of his poverty, than an illiterate man should omit praying because of his grammar. When we consider giving as worship, then we see this matter in its true relations. Exercise unto godliness is incomplete without a liberal hand in God's name.

But besides these common acts of worship in the assembly, there are others that appertain to the more general life of the church. Visiting the poor and suffering is expressly recorded by the Spirit as a mark of pure religion. Our Saviour emphasizes this in his picture of the judgment. How is it that half the Christians in the world never think of this exercise? How many leave it to benevolent societies, or agents, or ministers, forgetting that it is a personal duty that no one can set aside without directly disobeying the Lord Jesus. God means your graces to grow by your contact with the suffering, by your ministry to the sick and sorrowing, by your sympathizing relief brought opportunely to the garret of the destitute. How can you refuse God's method and prosper? Are you afraid that such visiting will oblige you to give money? Then let that be an argument for your going. You need just that grace. Do n't say you have no means to give, when you can wear rings and necklaces and diamonds. Try the virtue of selling a diamond pin and giving the proceeds to the needy, making the poor widow's heart to leap with joy. It may be the grandest step in Christianity you ever took, since you were converted. When you have learned how to visit the afflicted systematically, and how to comfort them with substantial kindness personally in the name of Jesus, you will have opened a new fountain of delight for yourself, such as you little dreamed of in the days of your selfish isolation. You will look more like Jesus than you ever did before. Go modestly, not as if you were a superior going to see an inferior, for you are not; and go cheerfully, in the love of the Master, and go tenderly with concern for the sick or sad one, and go with the Scripture on your lips and a purse in your pocket, and go calmly and not in a hurry, remembering that this too is worship. Let every Christian engage in this personal visiting, man and woman. I think if this rule of Christ were obeyed, it would teach us to be less extravagant in our expenditures for selfish ends, to be less dashing in our costume, to be less thoughtful for our petty pleasures, in short, it would raise us to a higher, nobler level, nearer the angels and nearer to God. Suppose we try it just for a month, and see how it results.

Another form of Christian exercise unto godliness is found in teaching the word. The error that ordained men are alone to teach God's word is one of Satan's admirable devices to block the wheels of evangelization

There are indeed some who by their acquirements are fitted for a peculiar (and in some respects a higher) style of teaching. They have studied carefully, and under experienced guides, the original languages of Scripture, and have thoroughly digested the statements of revelation in whatever of system divine things are capable of sustaining to finite intellects. On these men the appointed agents of the church put their seal of approbation, that the church may have confidence in them as called of God to be pastors and teachers. But this by no means exhausts the teaching of the church. There is to be teaching in the family, and teaching out of the family, whether it be in the Sunday-school or neighborhood visiting. The Bible is to be opened and its precious promises spread out before the child, the sick patient, or the friend of whatever sort; and for this high function every converted soul is capable. It needs no Greek or Hebrew, nor does it require "the laying on of the hands of the presbytery." It demands only a pious heart and an overflowing love. When you have read a portion of the word, and pondered it, and been illumined and warmed by the new rays of truth, store up your treasure for another's benefit, and seek an opportunity to enrich a friend. Let no Christian fail to be a teacher of the word in some form and way as regularly and systematically as possible. The converse of the question in the second of Romans, is in perfect analogy with the gospel scheme: "Thou that art taught thyself, teachest thou not another?" The knowledge you possess of the Word of God is enough to enlighten many a dark heart. Can you rightfully hide your light under a bushel-measure? When God entered your heart, did he not make you a truth-bearer? What have you to show for your commission? Where is the work you have wrought? To whom have you taught the word of God? With what child of sin or of sorrow have you read the pages that minister heavenly comfort and instruction? Has not your Christian life been wholly or greatly defective in this duty? Can you not trace many of your own symptoms of spiritual unhealthiness to this lack? Is not your want of interest *in* and comfort *from* the Bible owing to your failure in making it known to others? The Sunday-school teacher occupies a position of growth. He receives quite as much as he gives; I think *more*. We cannot overestimate the value of well-ordered Sunday-schools for the training of both old and young in the church. And what is true eminently of the well-ordered Sunday-school is true of every form of systematic Bible instruction. It is not only in the preparation that is necessary for the lesson, which increases the knowledge of divine things, but it is in the contact with a living soul receiving great truths that the teacher obtains his own benefit. The truths are enlarged in his own soul as he sees them impressing another; and his sympathy runs with the pupil by awakening his own impressions anew.

Another form of Christian exercise unto godliness is found in utterance at the prayer-meeting. It is not to be expected that any man can arise and speak to edification among God's people without due preparation. The notion that any man is like a fountain, and it needs only the turning of a fawcet and the stream of useful speech will flow, is a mistaken one. The men who appear to speak *impromptu* and with ease, are those who have thoroughly prepared themselves. This thorough preparation is the secret of their ease in utterance. The fault in our prayer-meetings is that Christians do not prepare themselves to speak to edification, and hence do not offer a word. Their inability to speak they think to be a natural lack, and hence they leave the duty to others, when their inability is simply owing to their neglect of preparation. What is to be prepared? Not an exhaustive essay. Not a sermon. Not a fine piece of rhetoric. If it were any of these, inability might be pleaded rightfully on the part of many. But that which is to be prepared is simply a fact-statement, as you would tell it to a friend, a word of personal experience, a view personally enjoyed of some passage of Scripture, anything that is brief and simple and calculated to warm or cheer the hearts of believers. If every Christian felt his duty in this respect, the leader of the meeting would not have to summon by name any particular member to guide the thoughts of the assembly, but only to designate which one of those that offered should take his turn to discharge this duty. This very readiness would add new life to the meeting, and increase its efficiency in all hearts. Diffidence in speaking to a hundred persons may be overcome by conscientious practice. Let the first words be few, and the simpler the better, and let the desire be to do one's part towards edifying the church. The diffidence will grow less at every utterance. Of course I do not refer to those exceptional cases where nervous disease is a very just excuse from this form of Christian exercise. In all these exercises of exhortation or instruction, brevity, point and simplicity must be insisted on, and these qualities will make it an easier duty to the conscientious soul? Where many are thus ready, we have the best guarantee against untimely dissertations, irrelevant harangues and empty wordiness, which ought to have no part in Christian assemblies.

Now, my fellow-believers, I have put before

you some of the ways in which the Lord calls each of us to exercise himself unto godliness in the midst of his church on earth. It remains for us to apply the truth by asking each himself the question, "Am I practising this system of spiritual strengthening? Am I taking this divinely-appointed means to preserve the vigorous vitality of my heaven-born life?"

One of the most frequent and plausible arguments against the practical adoption of these various forms of Christian exercise is the want of time. The mother's domestic duties, and the father's business duties are all-absorbing and leave no time for visiting or teaching the word, or preparing edifying words for the prayer-meeting, even if they allow time for attending that meeting. The answer to this favorite argument is perfectly simple. It is that our eternal interests are superior to all else, and that any plan of life which leaves them out and neglects their furtherance according to God's appointments, is radically wrong and cannot receive God's blessing. Moreover, I know active business men and excellent house-keeping ladies who *do* find abundant time to attend to all these spiritual exercises, and to whom the visitation of the poor, and sick, and afflicted is a most happy relief from their domestic or business duties. And, still again, those who make the excuse have plenty of time to visit their friends, to read their favorite books, to do a large amount of amateur shopping, and to take their drives and excursions. The want of time is not an excuse we shall dare to use before the judgment-seat of Christ. Our convictions there will be too clear that selfishness occupied the time that the Lord wanted.

Remember what we have before shown, that regular exercise of our spiritual man is as necessary for spiritual health as our bodily exercise is necessary for the right and sound use of our physical functions; that revealed truth received into the soul by faith, and nurtured by Christian companionship, must also be used in positive Christian activity toward others, if Christ is to be completely developed in us; and this, if we are Christ's, should be our one aim.

# CHAPTER VIII.

## THE SOUL'S EXERCISE: IN THE WORLD WITHOUT.

HAVING considered two spheres of opportunity for the regular exercise of our Christian graces, the one in the family and the other in connection with church organization, we turn now to a third, that which is presented in our business life. It will be borne in mind that this exercise is *unto godliness*—is a means ordained of God for the development of truth in us, to reject which is to consent to a stunted spiritual condition with all its consequences. Let this thought accompany all our investigations upon the subject.

Our life on earth is one and our character is one. We cannot separate our social life from our domestic life, or our business life from either. The principles which operate in one will operate in all. Selfishness and trickery in business will be found in the family as equally selfishness and deceit. A man may put on two faces, but he can have only one heart. As everything goes to make up our one character in life, so our one character will act upon everything in life. All exceptions to this rule are phenomenal only. A man who acts the tyrant in his family may appear to be affable and yielding in commercial circles, but it is only in appearance. The iron hand wears a velvet glove for policy's sake. Sometimes, perhaps, his cunning is off its guard, and the tyrant appears. Such slips form the eccentricities of some men that are so inexplicable to their fellows. A godly man can no more shut out his business life from his religion than the sun can refuse to shine in one direction. When it is attempted, the religion is proved, by that very fact, to be of a very low order. It is like a stream in the desert that the sands absorb before it can fertilize. I know this type of strange Christianity is found.

There are men who will meet with missionary boards and occupy positions of responsibility in the church, and yet go down to their office, store, or counting-room as thorough heathen, never saying a word to their clerks, or before their clerks, of the Kingdom of Christ; but, on the contrary, impressing their clerks and their customers with a sense of their hardness and unpitying severity, showing no sympathy or tenderness toward any, acting the part in real life of Shylock or Ralph Nickleby. What must be the effect of such a life upon the world in its estimate of evangelical religion? For the world does not read the Bible. It reads men. It sees the grand and leading firm of Messrs. Driver & Holdem. Mr. Driver built a large church in Driverville. He furnished the parsonage of the city church, of which he is a member. He gave the Sunday-school a noble library. He is chairman of the board for providing the destitute with the gospel. Alas! his gifts have harmed the church more than benefited it. They have made the Sunday-school superintendent and the church officers and the trustees and the minister to close their eyes and mouths against his worldliness, and so to join hands with it. They always have a pleasant smile for Mr. Driver, although they know that he has just been engaged in a large "cornering operation." And as for Mr. Holdem, the partner, he is the man who makes such a beautiful prayer; who instituted the daily prayer meeting, and sends the "Journal of Missions" gratuitously to ten thousand persons. He is also the man that broke the heart of a simple-minded Christian man from Kansas, who came to his store to ask aid for a struggling band of Christ's people there, by thrusting him violently out of his premises. He is the man who took advantage of the usury laws to give his creditors the go-by. He is the man who sells property to weak purchasers, so as to foreclose and regain the property with the first payment as clear gain. All Wall street knows Messrs. Driver & Holdem; and although they are worth five millions at least, all Wall street watches them as carefully in any business transaction as it would watch a state-prison graduate.

What idea, I ask, will Wall street have of

the Church of Jesus Christ, as it sees that church through the firm of Driver & Holdem? And what real benefit do such men confer upon the church by their gifts, given as they are to blind others and their own consciences to their own heathenish character? It is high time that the church should prefer straitness and poverty rather than entangling alliances with such traitors to the truth.

We have very strong doubts whether Driver & Holdem were ever converted. We are forced to believe them hypocrites and nothing else. But there are others, of whose underlying faith in Christ we have no reason to doubt —men who have given satisfactory evidence, in crises of their lives, that they saw the unseen and eternal. But these men leave all manifestation of their religion outside of their places of business. They are like automata, moving mechanically through their routine, but all soulless in the presence of their business companions. They defend their conduct by saying, "Only business in business hours." I take issue with their axiom. Where did they get it? Is it in God's word? Is there not another sort of axiom in that blessed volume, that says, "Whether ye eat or drink, or *whatever ye do*, do all to the glory of God"? That axiom tells me that my godliness should ooze out at every pore of my daily duties, when I'm selling silks or buying molasses, not by assumed cant and weak platitudes, but by an honest, manly, Christian style of doing business that would sparkle with its true courtesy and consideration, and so commend the Christianity that lay behind it. A man of that stamp would know when to throw out the word in season for God; when to correct firmly evil language or conduct; when to encourage a desponding clerk; when to have a private interview with some one dependent upon him and whom he could counsel as a father. Such a one would have no lack of opportunity to let his light shine in his place of business without harming an iota of his commercial or monetary interests.

In some of the large Christian firms of England, where scores and hundreds of clerks are employed, regular morning prayers are established, and the head of the house reads and expounds a passage of Scripture daily to all, and on Sunday he has them all with their families in a Sunday evening Bible-class. This is a noble example. The relations thus established between employers and employed are of the right sort. Holy sympathies are created and nurtured between them, and they are all led in their business to serve the Lord. Who will brave public opinion and dare, for Christ's sake, to begin such a custom here? We are too great cowards to be Christians. We are always wondering what the world will say; and if we surmise that it would ridicule a projected action on the side of God and truth, we take care to be very quiet, perhaps hoping secretly that some one else will do it and meet the brunt, and then we can safely follow. Why should it not be known and said of our Christian merchants, tradesmen, and mechanics, "These men fear God and serve him in all their business. An atmosphere of truth and godliness surrounds their lives"? Is not this the only reputation a Christian ought to have in the world? Why should we have to search the church records to discover if A. B. is a

Christian? Is that letting one's light shine? Is that presenting oneself a living sacrifice to God? Is that standing with one's loins girt about with truth? Oh, how unlike these Scriptural portraits of the true Christian are those who exclude their religion from their places of business! We forget that Christianity is not a performance, but a life. If it were a performance, we might crowd the work into certain hours or days and leave the rest free. But it is a life, and if the life is vigorous and healthy, it cannot be eclectic in its exhibitions. It must overflow. The Christian business men we have just described are not pointed out by the commercial world as cheats and large-scale robbers. They do not belong to the class of Driver & Holdem. But their influence on Christianity is perhaps quite as evil. Those worldly men who happen to know their church-membership must consider religion, as seen in them, a very subordinate and insignificant affair. It is by no means as important as business and money. And so these worldly men are supported in their theory of putting off all thoughts of personal religion to a dying day. Those who are not aware of the professed Christianity of these ashamed believers are injured in another way. They see their moral and upright lives, and conclude that Christianity is of no more use than a fifth wheel to a coach. "Here are men as good as anything we wish to see. They do not lie and steal. They are honorable men and keep their engagements. They are respected by all, and trusts are reposed in them to any extent. What more does man want?" Now the real foundation of the commercial uprightness of these men is in their Christian faith. Men may be commercially upright who are not Christians, (although, generally, that sort of uprightness will not bear a very rigid microscopic examination,) but in these cases to which we refer the correct commercial life is really the result of Christian faith, and it is disloyalty to God to hide that connection. It confirms multitudes in endeavoring to go on in life without God. It is a tacit testimony for irreligion. When we think how much of a man's life is spent in his place of business, it is startling to think of this exclusion of religion from the business field. It is virtually banishing religion from three-quarters of one's waking life. We can see at a glance how fearfully prejudicial it must be to one's own religious experience; what a desert it must make of personal piety. Imagine a tree with the sap removed from three-quarters of it, or a man's body with all signs of life confined to a quarter of it. What kind of vigor would there be in that tree or in that man?

I know there rises up as a general objection to the visible presence of a religious life in business the fear of the charge of hypocrisy. The fear of hypocrisy is a very right one. We ought to dread hypocrisy. It is the worst of sins. It is the lie unto God as unto man. Our Saviour used words of fierce indignation, not against the publicans and harlots, but against the hypocrites. But the fear of hypocrisy and the fear of *the charge* of hypocrisy are different things. We ought not rashly and unreasonably to lay ourselves open to a false charge, but sometimes we are obliged to, if we would perform our duty before God. Daniel's praying might have been looked upon as sheer hypocrisy, its motive being considered a desire to show his independence of the king; but that possibility would not stop Daniel's praying. Doubtless many charge Christians with hypocrisy in going to church, but that charge will not warrant a relinquishment of this high duty. If introducing living religion into your place of business is going to bring upon you the charge of hypocrisy, stand the charge like a Christian, so long as it is a lying charge, so long as you know you are *not* a hypocrite. I know there is a cheap twaddle that goes for religion with some shallow pates, or shrewd pates, as the case may be. It is very disgusting and every manly heart is repelled by it. But do not reject the pure gold because of the counterfeit. Be discreet, use common sense, be natural, and then be bold and independent. Do what you know to be right in the sight of God, and force those around you into respect. Let the community as little expect you to be a heathen in your store as in your church.

I have looked on the influence of such exercise of your spiritual life upon your own personal growth in grace, for that is our subject

—the means of developing the healthy Christian. My allusions to influence and opinion without have been only to illustrate this subjective condition. If it were not for this circumscription of subject, it would be easy to show the immense importance of a positive Christianity in our business men in business hours for the spread of the truth. I could enlarge on the channels opened by commercial intercourse for gospel currents, and the power of young men nurtured under such commercial training for the spiritual welfare of the race. But my design precludes this direction of thought. It is the subjective influence we are now studying. We are noting that the law of Christian growth forbids the repressing of the exercise of any of the divine gifts, at the peril of the spiritual welfare; that a Christian who withholds the demonstration of his faith in any one department of his life thereby diseases his spiritual nature, dishonoring God while he reduces his own capacity for the higher joys of the life of faith. The Lord as our shepherd leads us into green pastures and beside waters of rest, but our perversity makes the landscape a desert. We move among untried opportunities and have no right to murmur at our barren and unsatisfactory experience. The business life of the Christian might be to him a well-spring of spiritual refreshing. He might identify it with all that is holy and divine. Every business connection might contain a golden thread of godly recognition, and the purest and most truly religious associations might cluster around the buyings and sellings of trade. It is because Christian men have so long worked upon an opposite and false principle that this proposition looks fairly startling. If they begin again from God to mould their business life anew, they would see that there is no conflict between religion and business, as they have practically taught, but that the religion of Jesus sanctifies business and belongs to it, as much as to the social and domestic sides of human life. And when they have made this discovery, they will then make the still more astonishing discovery that business sanctifies *them*. God has called no disciple to a duty that is not sanctifying, if used aright. If we are not growing spiritually from our daily occupations, we may be sure that we are very wrong somewhere; we are divorcing them from the spiritual life, and so virtually making our business a clandestine dealing with the enemy. It is such a false system which makes some Christians say, under stress of conscience, "I 'm going to keep in business only a few years, till I gain so much, and then I 'm going to serve the Lord more systematically and zealously." My brother, what is to hinder you from serving the Lord systematically and earnestly *in* your business? Why have to go out of it, in order to be a consistent Christian? Why not sanctify your business by erecting an altar in your counting-room? Your style of speech suggests that your business has some crooked ways in it that would not bear inspection. If this be so, I the more earnestly appeal to you to cast out the demon from your store and let the Lord Jesus, *your* Lord Jesus, ever be by your side, at your ledger, behind your counter, in conference with your customer, so that you may exercise yourself unto godliness in all your doings.

# CHAPTER IX.

## THE SOUL'S EXERCISE: IN CHRISTIAN SOCIETY.

I HAVE endeavored to show that the society of believers is the fresh air to a believer's piety, purifying his Christ-life from the false additions which accrue either from a morbid isolation on the one hand, or from worldly intimacies on the other. My purpose now is to show that this society of believers is one of the appropriate spheres in which he is to exercise himself unto godliness. He is not only to be a recipient of good by these relations, but to be also a giver of good. And by the society of believers I do not mean an alliance with believers in acts of worship, a formal connection in what are known as church relations, but a *social life* with those who have the same hope, the same salvation, the same Christ. The necessity of forming such a relationship, the breaking up of many common habits which it implies, the complete abjuring of a trifling world, the willingness to be considered peculiar, and contrasted by that world—all these points we have already considered. It remains for us now only to consider the forms in which a Christian may exercise his graces in such a godly society thus constituted.

1. My first observation has respect to *conversation.* I use the word in its modern sense, for verbal intercourse. God has endowed us with speech as the medium of communion and communication between soul and soul. By it the observation, logic and imagery of the mind are projected into a condition that can be grasped and used by another. Ideas that otherwise would be vague and formless, are defined by this high faculty of man, and by their very definition give birth to new ideas, which are formative in their

turn, and so through language the mind grows in knowledge and wisdom. The beasts that are intended to remain stationary in their rudimental knowledge, creatures of an instinct that never grows, need little language; but man, born to have dominion over the beasts and with capacity to partake of the divine, possesses alone of earth's inhabitants this grand endowment by which his progress may be insured, and his alliance with supernal beings is established. The prostitution of such a faculty to low and trifling ends is a fearful abuse of the divine grace and purpose. It is not only where lying and slander defile the tongue that speech is degraded, it is not only where a wicked heart makes the tongue the instrument of crime, but it is also where this noble faculty becomes the agent of what the apostle has called "foolish talking." Enter any ball-room, pass from group to group, and note the conversation that is common to all. Is the twittering of swallows more vacant? Petty scandal, commonplace compliments, threadbare wit—these are the loftiest terms we can use to designate the bubbles of prattle to which men and women degrade speech in their principal social reunions, for which they make their especial preparations. In this style of school the mass of what is most whimsically called "refined society" obtains its education, and so this senseless chatter becomes one of the characteristics of "refined society." Any proposition to elevate the tone of conversation is at once hailed as an audacious attempt to encroach upon the prerogative of fashion, and a desire to make everything sombre and dull. The lazy dawdle of the drawing-room magnifies every effort to convert it into something sensible as a presentation of the higher mathematics, or Hebrew roots. People forget that it is just as easy to talk sense as nonsense, if they will only form the habit. Sense does not mean profound study. Sense may be very simple. A peasant can talk sense. And a Christian *ought to.*

If we leave the ball-room and follow the ordinary social visitor from house to house, we find no higher standard of colloquy in general use. Dreary commonplace or unwholesome gossip meets us everywhere. If we take to the street, we find a shrill treble of laces and ribbons, and a running base of dollars and dividends, as the almost universal music of conversational life.

Now, in direct opposition to all this, the believer is to use this large field of opportunity for the exercise of his religious acquirements. Not that each conversation of a Christian is to be a sermon, or that he is never to talk without a testimony direct for Christ. Such a method would defeat its own end. But he is to be so full of the great fact of Christ's redeeming love, that he will naturally and easily turn anything in conversation to the advantage of the grand subject. Moreover, his whole manner of treating all other subjects will be that of a Christian, so that he will show his believing soul even when he makes no verbal allusion to the truths of revelation. He will avoid words and phrases, very common in the world which smack of profanity or infidelity, and wlll not allow him self for a moment to descend to tattle or twaddle. He can be humorous without being either low or flat, preserving a religion and dignity even in his pleasantry.

If a soul is full of Christ's love, this high character of speech will not be a difficult task or exhibit the appearance of stiffness, but will be the natural effluence of its affections. It does not banish fun, but folly. It does not seek solemnity, but solidity.

At times, indeed, the Christian will be solemn in his speech. Where the right opportunity offers he will, remembering his high commission of God, speak to his friend or companion of the things of eternity. This responsibility is but little understood, or, at least, but little accepted among the majority of Christians. It should occupy a large part of their thoughts, not as an unwelcome and inconvenient load, but as a glad duty for Christ's sake. It is a sad reflection that so few of Christ's people are known by their conversation, and that thus the influence of the church is curtailed, and strange inferences are drawn by the world with regard to the value of the gospel. A Christian who thus refuses to testify for Christ is really testifying against him. Many Christians have dated their first true rapture in their religious experiences from the time when they dared to open their mouths boldly for the Lord in conversation with their friends. The breach in the wall of reserve has proved a road for heavenly delights to enter in.

But not only in speech with the unregenerate, but in conversation with converted souls a great revolution should be inaugurated among us. Why should not Christ's people, when they meet together, speak of him? Why should their dear Saviour be unmentioned, as if he were dead, or as if his name had an ill omen in its use? Why should not conversation among Christians naturally gravitate toward the great themes of salvation. Remember the suggestive passage in the prophet Malachi, "They that feared the Lord spake often one to another, and the Lord hearkened and heard it, and a book of remembrance was written before him for them that feared the Lord, and that thought upon his name. And they shall be mine, saith the Lord of hosts, in that day when I make up my jewels; and

I will spare them, as a man spareth his own son that serveth him." By such frequent conversation on divine things, they are kept fresh and efficient in the soul, and one of the best securities against worldliness is established. The exercise is "unto godliness." In order to such a habit we must have in the first place a deeper and more living interest in divine things, for out of the abundance of the heart the mouth speaketh; and then we must have a more familiar acquaintance with God's word, so that its texts should ever rise in our minds as the subjects of our remark. The lack of these two qualifications probably lies back of our failure in this important department of spiritual exercise, and our reform must begin there. As in every characteristic action of a true Christianity, so here we see that a real separation from the world, a clear and seen distinction, is the will of God concerning us.

2. The second method in which our Christian life should exercise itself in society is in *mutual service*. It was said of Dorcas, she was "full of good works." Our social life

might be almost made up of this holy material. Help is wanted by everybody every day in some form, help for body and help for soul. There are little disappointments to be assuaged, little obstacles to be cleared away, little provocations to be soothed down, little sorrows to be comforted, little hardships to be alleviated, besides the great evils to which we are all exposed; and the Christian soul ought to be ever-ready and watching to minister to these constantly-recurring wants of our fellows. It is not only the actual relief in external matters that is brought about by such a healthy system of "bearing one another's burdens," but there is a higher ministry to the sympathies of the soul. The magnetism of Christian friendship renews the desponding or disordered heart, and our oneness in Christ is made manifest. Such a manifestation is a heavenly balm, communicating peace and strength. The adroitness of a Christian perception will discover the secret springs of blessing, and lead out their refreshing streams. It is as a society founded on these principles of sympathy and active love that the Scriptures portray the church of Jesus, forming so marked a contrast with the world, where self-display and self-aggrandizement assume perhaps a cloak of courtesy in the intercourse of society, but where, notwithstanding, each soul is isolated and, according to the paradoxical proverb, even charity is cold.

There can be no doubt that the social nature and requirements of man are better met and satisfied by an intercouse that has mutual relief and benefit as one of its constituent elements, than by one which has only the connections of outward habit or fashion as its essential power. It is a mistake to suppose that idleness or vacuity of mind and heart has anything restful in it; and hence the pleasures of worldly society, far from satisfying, leave a sense of dreariness and loneliness and weariness upon the spirit. It is a species of intoxication, attractive, even fascinating, for a moment, but leaving its sting behind. It is only where the affections have instituted a ministry, a permanence of mutual service, that the soul really rests and is refreshed. And such a permanent institution we will vainly look for outside the influences of God's Word and the Holy Spirit. It is not a native growth from man's selfish nature. It should be the glory of the church of Christ to exhibit this healthy action of a ceaseless sympathy between its members, and in such activities the Christian should, as we have seen, find the very atmosphere he breathes.

It is a matter of deep concern that we find Christ's church so little fulfilling the designs of its Lord. Just as the ancient Jews let a familiar intercourse with the idolatrous nations steal away their hearts from God, and so, under the claims of business or falsely-established relationships, let slip one by one the distinctive features of their holy state, until the severest chastisements were necessary to purge them of their corruption and bring them back to God; so the church of Jesus now is, by its false partnerships with an unbelieving world, giving up the divine methods of its true life, and yielding itself to the pernicious, though often plausible, habits of a Christless society, using the arguments and reaching the conclusions which are foreign to the revelation of God, and directly antagonistic to all growth in grace. The deceitful allurements of riches, the attractions of position, the taste for low pleasure are more potent than the commands of God, the consistency of Christ's truth, the beauty of holiness and the raptures of divine communion. Can we see the sad repetition of Israel's sin without shuddering in expectation of Israel's fearful chastisement? Is God going to leave his people to corrupt themselves? Will he not vindicate his truth, while he seeks their recovery?

Some are ready to say that this is a puritanic view of things, and by that they would mean that we are too stern in our judgment, and too strict in our requirements. But to the law and to the testimony! Let them decide the question for us. "Be ye holy as I am holy," is the great command of God to you and me, and the way to obey it is in Jesus Christ by a life of faith and faith's ready obedience. Does the prevailing form of Christian society conform to this standard? Is not the ordinary Christian life of to-day a round of worldliness with a dash of legalistic religion thrown in to satisfy conscience? Are not many Christians as mad after money and display as the ungodly?

I speak with emphasis of this sad condition of the church, because reform here must really be the basis of all change for the better. Of what use is anything else to a body, if it breathe foul air? Neither food nor exercise can save it from disease, if it is inhaling poison into the lungs. And if a believer remain in full communion with the world, he has no power to exercise himself healthfully. The sphere of healthy exercise is away from him. Give him a social life among God's people, and then he can exercise his Christian energies to his increase in godliness; and then too the Word of God will nourish him aright and Christ be developed in his soul. The great want of the church is, therefore, separation from the world. Every healthy demand of recreation or amusement can be found in the Christian society to which God's word directs us, while the actions of such a society in works of mutual comfort, encouragement, and help will prove themselves a source of permanent pleasure, which has no counterpart in the activities of a worldly society. The unsatisfying character of worldly society is keenly and sadly felt when its ephemeral excitement is over. In spite of our efforts to the contrary, it proves hollow and mocking. Momentary triumphs and ultimate defeat of self mark the history of the soul that seeks its pleasure in anything short of the divine; but the soul that seeks its pleasure in God and his people, that finds its delight in giving and receiving the living sympathy of truth and holiness, occupies a sphere of perennial sunshine. God himself is the minister of its pleasures, and he never fails. Feverish excitement is exchanged for calm repose, in accordance with the promise, "Thou wilt keep him in perfect peace whose mind is stayed on thee." As the world does not give the happiness, so the world cannot take it away. It is out of its reach. The chains of bondage to the world are broken, and the soul is free. The unbeliever, as his name implies, does not believe that such a life of happiness exists, and with him I do not now attempt to argue; but you, my believing friend, *know* that this truly happy life is within your reach, and you ought to know that your conformity to the world is your only hinderance to its enjoyment. Is it in vain that I bid you listen to your dear Saviour, saying, "I have chosen you out of the world;" "I have chosen you that ye should go and bring forth fruit;" and again, through his apostle, "Walk as children of light; "have no fellowship with the unfruitful works of darkness"? Is it in vain that Christ's own people are urged to break the alliance with a world that hates Christ? I beseech you not to let mere consequences come into consideration, when the Saviour's command is so explicit and reiterated. Exercise yourselves unto godliness by a speech trained in Christian conversation, and by social intimacies that shall further your spiritual health, and so supply your spiritual joy. Cast off, as Satan's chains, the false excuses about the needs of youth and the requirements of recreation and the demands of fashion, and trust Jesus and Jesus only, as you obey his commands, letting consequences take care of themselves. Then yours will be a symmetrical Christ-life, and the spiritual diseases which disfigure and desolate the church of Christ will leave you to stand before God his noblest work, *a healthy Christian.*

# CHAPTER X.

## THE SOUL'S EXERCISE: IN PERSONAL CULTURE.

THE last sphere for the exercise of our Christian life, to which I would refer, is that of *direct personal culture*. We have considered the opportunities offered in the family, in our church relations, in our business, and in our social connections. We now come to the man himself. There is a direct work for himself, as well as an indirect work through his relation to others. While man is made for others, and the great part of his life must be shaped amid associational forces, and while the Christian's life is no exception to the rule but must be very largely intermingled with the lives of others, and in this intermingling he finds the elements of a successful and healthy growth, still there must be times of separation from the great without, a shutting up of the soul to its own converse, or rather a withdrawing to be with God alone.

The active, nervous life which we lead in this land and age has proved inimical to this phase of Christian experience. The Church of Christ in our country is an active, bustling church, but it cannot be called a meditative church; and so personal Christian experience is more apt to assume the energetic than the contemplative form. I speak of a ripe and healthy experience.

We escape some great evils, it is true, by this style of development, but we also lose very great advantages. The evils we escape are those of morbid self-inspection, which are the spiritual diseases of honest monasteries and nunneries; the vain attempt incessantly to analyze our own hearts and know them, which ends either in conceit or despair; the critical examination of every motive and thought; the dissection and measurement of every sin and every grace in us—all which is meddling with the incomprehensible, a very vain, puzzling, and calamitous business. These are great evils, indeed, which the driving, Jehu-like Christian is not liable to suffer from; but there are advantages in temporary isolation, whose loss he ought not to endure composedly. A meditative Christian need not be a self-scrutinizing Christian. He may look at his life historically, without dissecting his own heart. The latter work is God's only. "Search me, O God," is the psalmist's cry. He did not know how to search himself. But while we commit this search of our hearts to God, our past lives lie before us as an historic fact, which we can safely contemplate, as we would a landscape or a numerical account. We ought to make a balance-sheet from time to time in our religious life, as we do in our pecuniary concerns. Have I treated my fellow-men as a Christian ought to, last week, or last month? Have I been searching God's truth with more eagerness? Have I been an example to my family and friends? Have I sought the welfare of others? Have I been regular in my use of the means of growth which God has provided? Questions like these have nothing sickly in them. They are sound, honest questions, to be answered according to historic fact—very different questions from such as these: "Was my motive *perfectly* pure when I gave that dollar to the poor man? Did I *sufficiently* weigh the words of my prayer last evening? Is my heart ready to make *every* sacrifice for Christ?" It is this latter style of questions whose answer involves the analysis of a labyrinth, which makes melancholy and very useless Christians. Books that encourage such an unscriptural self-dissection ought to be burned. But the contemplation of our past life, its outline of hill and valley, the way God's mercy has led us, and our own failures and progress—this is an easy and wholesome duty. The whole Bible urges us to it. "See what I have done for you, and see how little you have used your advantages," is the virtual cry of God to his people all through the history of his church. There is not one of us who has not a history replete with wonders of Divine grace. By looking back carefully we can see how God has led us by ways we knew not; how trial has borne its peaceable fruits of righteousness; how dangers have been thwarted and thrust aside by the interposition of providential trifles; how our own errors have brought us injury, and yet how God has ever overruled that injury for our good; how, in short, our whole life has been a constant discipline of an affectionate Heavenly Father. Now, this profiting view cannot be enjoyed while in the push and crowd of busy life. It demands retirement and time. The mind must be quiet, so that the memory can act soberly and systematically. Yet very few Christians apparently feel the importance of this tranquil hour of meditation. Perhaps they consider it a luxury they can forego, rather than a necessity they must seize. They hear David say, "I will meditate of all thy work," Ps. 77:12; and again, "I meditate on all thy works; and muse on the work of thy hands," Ps. 143:5; and they think that was well for David, so eminent a saint, but they, alas! are too much driven in life for such a high enjoyment. Perhaps, however, they deem it neither necessity nor luxury, indeed think nothing about it, but *carelessly* lose the benefits of this means of grace.

Another subject of meditation is God's revealed word. The psalmist is full of this. "In God's law doth he meditate day and night" (Ps. 1:2)—this is in his description of a godly man. "I will meditate in thy precepts and have respect unto thy ways;" "My hands also I will lift up unto thy commandments, which I have loved, and I will meditate in thy statutes;" "Mine eyes prevent the night watches, that I might meditate in thy word;" "I love thy law—it is my meditation all the day;" "Thy testimonies are my meditation." These are some of the utterances of the godly king himself, and here we see the secret of his maintaining his integrity amid the fearful temptations of wealth and absolute power. There is infinite food for thought in the Bible. We must do more than read the Bible. A Christian should be like the clean beasts of the law, and spend times of rest in chewing the cud. The word read should be brought up by memory for new and more complete digestion, and only in this process can God's word be said to be known. This, it will be marked, is a different thing from studying the Scriptures, to which an allusion has been made under another head. This is the revolving of the studied word in our thoughts, so as to fit it to our own cases and apply it to our own lives. *Studying the Word* implies search with every help of commentary, encyclopædia, dictionary, and Scripture comparison that can be obtained; but *meditating on the Word* is the use of the knowledge of the Word thus gained in all its relations to ourselves. This meditation on the Word naturally combines with meditation on our past lives, and thus adjustment and improvement are suggested. One of the grandest forms of this meditation on the Word is found in the review of Christ's marvellous work for us. To follow the Son of God from heaven to earth, to see him a babe at the inn-stable of Bethlehem, a youth at Nazareth, a teacher, wonder-worker, and lover of souls in Galilee and Judea, to witness his agony in the Garden and on the Cross, to behold him bursting the bars of the grave, and to look after his receding figure in the clouds over Olivet, going to prepare a place for us—these are enjoyments of the meditative hour which impress their lasting lessons on the heart and life. There, too, we ponder on the love that wrought all this, the yearning love of Jesus for his own ransomed ones; and there, in an emphatic manner, do we talk with Him, really present to our consciousness. This talking with Jesus is prayer—is the confiding speech of a child and not the cry of a stranger. It is not a shriek for help, but a gentle use of a perpetual help afforded in our Lord. Prayer is too often practically considered as merely an appeal to mercy, and so we who are Christ's are dishonoring him by constantly doing over our first works. If we are in Christ, his mercy is vouchsafed to us—we are already enveloped in his grace. Its blessed provisions are secured to us by the blood of the covenant. It is true that all we receive is based on his wondrous mercy, but the prayer of a believer should not be merely the cry for mercy, but a child's unbosoming to a Father. It is a holy communion with the dearest of friends, a putting out of the hand to receive his divine gifts, the very luxury of dependence upon his bountiful love. It is painful to see how some Christians take the command to "pray without ceasing" to be an order from heaven to cry out continually, "Lord, have mercy upon us!"—a very proper cry for the inquirer, the convicted soul, the seeking sinner, but as utterly out of place for the chief prayer of the believer as would have been the cry, "Make me as one of thy hired servants," on the part of the prodigal, after he had been welcomed and received as a dear son into his father's house. If our experiences lead us to use only the cry for mercy, it proves a very low view of our privileges and a very low condition of our piety. False churches have encouraged this method of keeping back the believer in everlasting babyhood, by which system priestcraft has attained its earthly ends. We are, of course, always to ask forgiveness for our daily errors, but it is to be as a child says to his father, "Father, forgive me that fault," not as an alien coming now for the first to receive pardon for a sinful soul. The whole wretched figment of penance is constructed on this false principle, ignoring Christ's atonement once for all, and making, after every sad lapse of a believer, a new entrance into grace necessary. Superficial observers may think this is laying a proper emphasis on sin, but it is just the reverse: it is making sin a matter of so little moment that a human regimen can cure it, while at the same time it belittles God's grace, which, if received into the soul, is an enemy to sin and takes precedence there before the eye of God. God's grace in the heart is a principle which enables the believer to contend against sin, and which is both encouragement and pledge of his success; and to make a believer begin anew, as a convicted sinner, to cry for mercy, is to shut him out from that gracious advantage and fill him with despair. Let us put prayer where Jesus puts it. It begins with "Our Father." The rest all flows from that. When prayer is thus viewed, lifted up from the low position it holds in so many minds, and made a transporting communion with God, then the command to pray without ceasing is equivalent to a divine authorization to walk with God all the time and to enjoy a heavenly happiness in the midst of all our earthly vicissitudes. The command shows that we can carry the prayerful spirit with us in all our business of life, but still there must be opportunities secured from life's business, where the *whole* attention of the soul may be given to this sublime exercise. The laws of our spiritual nature demand this, as well as the command of our Saviour concerning *closet prayer*. We cannot trust our souls for any spiritual exercise in its full force while the mind is absorbed in any external business. The soul that thinks it can catch its food as it goes will grow lean. There is such a thing as cultivating everybody's garden but our own.

Daniel's "three times a day" and David's "seven times a day" were stated periods of retirement for prayer and communion with God of men who were overwhelmed with the affairs of state, fully as busy as the busiest man in any commercial city. There these holy men gained the beauty of their spiritual character. When prayer is regarded in this its high and true character, there can be no formality, no legalistic dragging in the exercise.

One other private exercise of the Christian life I wish to mention, which, however, has a public side. I refer to the use of the Lord's Supper. The communion of the Lord's Supper is not the communion of saints, but the communion of the body and blood of Christ. We *do* meet together and hold communion with one another at the same time, but the essence of the exercise is in our communion with our Lord, and hence the name. The Lord's Supper is the central exercise of Christ's Church. It is the emblematic service respecting the central fact of our redemption. It is the gospel in token. In the apostolic church, the Lord's Supper was partaken of every Lord's Day. Around it gathered the worship and instruction of the church. The apostle Paul, in his first epistle to the Corinthians, sets forth its prominence, while he guards it from perversion. It has been the fault of many Protestant bodies, in practical protest against the magical character which the Roman Church gave it, to diminish the real importance of the Eucharist as a means of grace, an ordained exercise of the Christian soul. We must avoid both extremes. On one hand we must recognize from Scripture that there is no mystic power in the elements or the minister—that there is no *material* grace or condemnation in the service, but that our faith in Jesus and his word gives it all its value to us, and our want of faith in Jesus and his word gives it all its power to harm us, as a holy exercise engaged in with a careless, God-defying spirit. Then, on the other hand, we must not treat it as a *mere* external service—to be used or not, as the whim may take us—of small account if we have the truth in our hearts. Our Saviour would not have instituted it if it was of small importance. Every thing he ordered is and must be of importance. He commanded it, and *therefore* there is grace to be found in it by a faithful soul, which it cannot afford to spare.

The Eucharist is, as its name signifies, a thanksgiving service. It is concentrated praise for redeeming love, or rather for an accomplished redemption. It is the glad reception of a pledge from God, and the kernel of the exercise is in the individual soul thus taking gladly and thankfully this pledge from the hand of God. There is no exercise more simple, none more imposing, none more profitable. It is not a form, but a power, and that power is realized through plain faith.

That a Christian should stay away from this communion is as unreasonable as that he should abandon prayer or the study of the word. If he stay away from fear, he is superstitious. If he stay away from worldliness, he is a backslider. In both cases he is abandoning a means of grace, and disobeying the express commands of his Lord. He should view it in its private character, in its relations to himself, as a means of direct personal culture in holiness, if he would rightly estimate his partaking or abstaining. When faith lays hold of Jesus in his ordinance—when, to use the apostle's phrase, we "discern the Lord's body"—then the Eucharist is a service of glory, a refreshing from the presence of the Lord.

We thus see that every believer has his own

soul to cherish, his own piety to cultivate, by a direct culture, as well as by his active relations with others, for which time must be used at whatever cost, and for neglect of which no excuse of worldly care can stand for a moment before the tribunal of God or the conscience, and which, moreover, will bring its own peculiar reward by a heavenly vantage over all the possible trials of life. It is the exercise which fits the soul for all other exercise. Without it, every aspect of the Christian life will be disfigured.

## A CLOSING WORD.

WE have endeavored to follow the analogy of the body, in treating of the soul, and to show what are the believer's spiritual food, air, and exercise, by the right use of which his spiritual life will be sound and vigorous, by which both the blood-system and nerve-system of the soul, the indwelling of Christ and the Holy Spirit, will be maintained as against the powerful adversaries of the divine life which are so abundant and besetting in this sin-smitten earth.

Truth is an exotic here. It must be preserved by extraordinary measures. The Lord bids his people to be ever watchful. The vigilance of faith has a divine guarantee. It will surely accomplish its end. But where there is consent to the world's style of life, the world's aims or the world's system of ethical law, there is the betrayal of the divine trust, the defilement of the holy place.

Our citizenship is in heaven. We confess we are strangers and pilgrims on the earth. They that say such things declare plainly that they seek a country. They desire a better country: that is, a heavenly. It is with this prospect in view, and in this *habit* of mind and heart, that we are called upon to preserve and nourish what the grace of God in Christ Jesus has bestowed upon us.

The children of Israel at Sinai received a complete law for their future habitation in Palestine. But while still in the desert they were to cherish that law, and use all that could be used in the wilderness-situation. So are we, fellow-Christians, furnished with a divine law in Christ for our heavenly home; but here, on our pilgrimage, is that law of holiness to be cherished and employed to the fullest possible anticipation of the perfected state. We are a separated people. Let us not break down the holy barriers our God has put up.

www.ingramcontent.com/pod-product-compliance
Lightning Source LLC
LaVergne TN
LVHW021402110826
845150LV00007B/1746

* 9 7 8 1 4 2 5 5 1 2 9 7 2 *